The Media Hates Conservatives

How It Controls the Flow of Information

by
Dale A. Berryhill

Huntington House Publishers

Huntington House Publishers
P.O. Box 53788
Lafayette, Louisiana 70505

Library of Congress Card Catalog Number
94-75121
ISBN 1-56384-060-X

Dedication

To the many hard-working
journalists who strive for objectivity and
fairness in their reporting, and who do not use
their positions to push their
personal agendas.

Contents

Sources and Acknowledgments

The research for this book involved four aspects. First, hundreds of hours were spent analyzing news coverage of the 1992 presidential campaign from the major media outlets—both print and electronic. Second, in order to add objective, statistical proof of media bias, dozens of studies conducted by journalism scholars and media watchdog groups were reviewed. Third, many secondary sources—ranging from books on the campaign to essays by journalists on the role of the media—were examined. Finally, several of the principles in the campaign were interviewed, including Torie Clarke, media spokesperson for the Bush-Quayle campaign, and Floyd Brown, creator of the notorious Willie Horton ad. The result, it is hoped, is an informative but also entertaining mixture of news analysis, campaign anecdotes, and statistics, all framed by the ongoing evaluation and self-evaluation of the media's role in the American political process.

Primary research for this book was conducted in the offices of Accuracy in Media, Inc., 4455 Connecticut Avenue, N.W., Suite 330, Washington, D.C., 20008. AIM is a conservative media watchdog group that is the nation's oldest and largest. Thanks go to Reed Irvine, Joseph Goulden, Don Irvine, and Sandy Schuhart for their assistance.

Secondary research was conducted at the Media Research Center, 113 South West Street, Alexandria, Virginia, 22314, another conservative watchdog group. Thanks to Brent Bozell, Tim Graham, and Annette Jarad.

Secondary research was also conducted at the Center for Media and Public Affairs, 2100 L Street, N.W., Suite 300, Washington, D.C., 20037, a nonpartisan research group. Thanks to Dr. Robert Lichter, Rich Noyse, and John Sheehan.

All three of these organizations publish newsletters and conduct studies of media bias. Much of the material presented in this book was originally reported by these organizations, and I thank them again for allowing me access to their materials. Those interested in further information on these organizations and their publications may write to them at the addresses above.

Finally, thanks to Jack Whittington and Dawn Langley for their assistance during my trips to D.C.

Chapter One

Whose Fault Is It, Anyway?

"George Bush had better watch out," I told my friends. "This guy is no Michael Dukakis. This guy is a political animal who was born to run." This was in the early months of 1992, when Bill Clinton was first emerging as the Democratic front-runner and most people knew little about him. But, I knew plenty. I grew up in Memphis, Tennessee, just across the river from Bill Clinton's Arkansas, and Arkansas political news often found its way into our newspaper. When Clinton was first elected governor, I was a political science major at Memphis State University and an intern to the Tennessee State Legislature. I knew all about this youngest-governor-ever, who had suffered a humiliating defeat for his second term, but who had found a way to remake himself in time to get reelected the next time around.

When Tennessee's own Al Gore, Jr.–a man groomed from childhood for a political career by his senator father–was added to the ticket, I repeated my warnings that Bush had better run a good campaign if he wished to be reelected.

Unfortunately for the Republicans, George Bush seemed genuinely unaware of the threat he faced. He waited until the primary season was well under way before deciding officially to run again. His campaign was poorly organized and directionless, failing from the beginning to respond adequately to Democratic charges. The deficit in the Bush camp became clear when Secretary of State James Baker first refused, then reluctantly agreed to come home from the Middle East to run the campaign. Baker was so uninvolved in the effort that his staff members posted notices of the rare "Baker sightings." As time went on, Bush's speeches grew more shrill and less weighty, until the final embarrassing days when he was reduced to referring repeatedly to his opponents as "bozos."

Anyone criticizing the media's role in the 1992 presidential election must begin with this undeniable fact: George Bush ran a lousy campaign. He has admitted as much himself, and conservative leaders agree that Bush lost a very winnable contest. Even the conservative Accuracy in Media, which had documented and publicized media bias throughout the campaign, admitted in its November issue that "Bush proved to be less skilled than his two opponents at utilizing . . . opportunities to take his message to the people."

Soon after the election, the Heritage Foundation sponsored a forum at which the editors of five conservative newspapers did a postmortem on the Bush campaign. As reported by Accuracy in Media, "The consensus was that Bush's loss was largely self-inflicted because of the sluggish economy, broken promises, the abandonment of Reaganism, and an inability to make Americans feel he really cared for them . . . [and] ineptness by the Bush media staff did not help his cause."

Credit must also be given to the savvy and efficient Clinton campaign. They cultivated the press, they hammered consistently at Bush's weak spots, and they took advantage of new technology, offering a toll-free number and even faxing responses to speeches at the Republican National Convention directly to the network news desks. Time and again, Clinton, Gore, and their media handlers simply refused to answer questions about damaging charges, deftly turning the subject back to the themes on which they knew they could win.

Torie Clarke, press secretary for the Bush campaign, acknowledges that the administration had failed to get its messages out to the public long before the campaign began. "Some great things were done in the domestic policy areas," she says, "but because they weren't in the White House spotlight, they didn't get into the media spotlight."

So What's the Problem?

If Bush ran a lousy campaign and Clinton ran a good one, why blame the media? The answer is that even with all these discrepancies between the two campaigns, Clinton's margin of victory was still only 5 percent. The question then becomes: What would have happened to that narrow margin had the media faithfully reported that more than twenty women came forward claiming to have had affairs with Bill Clinton? Or had they reported that Clinton had gotten Gennifer Flowers a government job by denying promotion to a black woman? Or had they reported that Clinton, unlike Quayle, really did break the law in order to avoid the draft? Or had they actually quoted the radical scholarship of Hillary Clinton? Or had they adequately publicized the improvement in the economy in the quarter that ended in September?

And, what would have happened had the treatment of the two candidates been equal? What if the media had blasted Bill Clinton's and Jesse Jackson's references to God in the same way they blasted George

Bush's? What if Democratic attacks had been labeled "negative" as were Republican attacks? What if Clinton's claim to be a "new Democrat" were greeted with the same skepticism as the Republicans' commitment to family values?

What if the media had paid as much attention to the splits in the Democratic party as it did to those in the Republican party?

Throughout this book you will learn of specific actions by those in the media to assist the Clinton campaign. You will see example after example of a suspicious failure in the investigative abilities of the media that usually prides itself on those abilities. You will hear reporters adopting the rhetoric of the Democratic campaign. You will even hear reporters, commentators, and producers lying outright.

Had the media remained neutral, Clinton's popularity would certainly have been reduced, possibly costing him the election. It is not, therefore, an exaggeration to suggest that Clinton won because the media cooperated in hiding or ignoring many facts about the Democrats while at the same time characterizing the Republicans in a variety of undesirable ways. While we can never know what would have happened had the media done its job properly, you will find in this book a convincing case that the media actually stole the election for the Democrats.

It should be understood, then, that this book is not about the candidates or their campaigns, but about how the media covered them. The question is not whether Bush lied about Iran-Contra or whether Clinton lied about the draft, nor is it about which man will make the better president. The question is what the media did. And, what the media did was to act as a cohesive, partisan political organization operating outside the law with no accountability.

The Facts and Figures

In February 1992, the Center for Media and Public Affairs conducted a study of the 401 election stories that ran on the network evening news programs between 3 January 1991 and the New Hampshire primary on 18 February 1992. According to the center's report, "President Bush received the worst press of any candidate . . . nearly three-to-one negative. Nearly three out of every four sources (73%) who evaluated Bush have criticized him. Of all the presidential candidates, only ex-Klansman David Duke (76% negative) received worse press than Bush." Even with the scandals that had erupted around him, Bill Clinton received 38 percent positive coverage, while Bush had received only 20 percent positive.

"As a group," continues the report, "the Democratic contenders are getting better press than their Republican counterparts–52% positive for the Democrats vs. 29% for the Republicans."

The center refers to predictions of the candidates' electability as "horse race" stories. "Early favorite Clinton received 100% positive horse race press in 1991." This dropped to 51 percent following the Flowers and draft allegations. But, by the New Hampshire primary, it was back up to 59 percent. Tsongas enjoyed 80 percent positive and Buchanan 62 percent positive, while Bush got only 47 percent positive. Amazingly, even David Duke had a 54 percent positive evaluation of electability at that time, although no one seriously thought he was electable.

"In debating Bush's [New Hampshire] prospects, the networks gave little notice to polls which showed Bush maintaining a lead over Buchanan in New Hampshire. Rather, they focused mainly on the president's declining national approval rating, and his prospects for the general election."

"During the first three weeks after the primaries ended, Clinton's horse race notices were 69% negative [following the scandals]. Since then, they have been 83% positive."

"Even during the week of the Republican convention, nearly two out of three assessments of Bush's prospects were negative, while three out of four judgements of Clinton's chances were positive."

Back in the 1988 primaries, the center reports, the Republican and Democratic contenders, as groups, received basically the same amount of positive coverage. "During the 1992 primaries, by contrast, Republicans faced criticism from three out of four sources (25% positive evaluations), while Democratic contenders received roughly balanced press (46% positive)."

Political scientists at Harvard's John F. Kennedy School of Government–no bastion of conservatism–examined coverage by the four major networks of the primaries from 1 February to 4 June (all dates in this book are 1992 unless otherwise indicated). "When we examine the overall tone of the stories about the candidates," their report states, "we see that all broadcast networks were more critical of President Bush than of any of the other five [primary] candidates."

Just before the election, the Center for Media and Public Affairs analyzed coverage after June, taking up where the Kennedy study left off. "Since June," read the center's report, "evaluations of Bush have run three-to-two negative, while assessments of Clinton have been evenly balanced." In the postprimary campaign, the Democratic ticket enjoyed a two-to-one advantage of positive press from nonpartisan sources (those not officially connected to a campaign) quoted on network news shows.

Tom Rosensteil reports that "of the 417 stories on Bush in the *Washington Post* and *New York Times* between 1 June and the Republican convention in mid-August, only twenty-three had a decidedly positive tone. More than 300 were negative." This is important because stories and columns from these two papers are syndicated and widely reprinted by local newspapers.

In the four years since 1988, a consensus had developed among the media that they needed to focus more on policy issues rather than on staged campaign events, horse race stories, and scandals. According to the Center for Media and Public Affairs, the media succeeded in this: policy issues were the most reported-on topic throughout 1992, with coverage up 66 percent from 1988. But, there was a distinct difference in how such issues were covered for the two leading candidates. "In contrast to Bush, Clinton's media profile was shaped more by his proposals and positions than his record in public office." Bush's record was discussed exactly three times more than his positions and proposals (27 percent to 9 percent of all discussions about Bush), while Clinton's positions and proposals were discussed over three times more often than his record. "On major issues such as education and the environment, the networks have provided almost no debate over Clinton's records or proposals."

During the summer months, evaluations of Bush ran three-to-two negative, while assessments of Clinton were evenly balanced. The gap between their running mates was far greater. Three out of four sources praised Al Gore, while two out of three criticized Dan Quayle.

During the general election (Labor Day to Election Day), comments by reporters were 71 percent negative toward Bush and only 54 percent negative toward Clinton. According to the Center for Media and Public Affairs, "Partisan Republican criticism of Clinton was balanced by praise from voters and pundits, while partisan Democratic criticism of Bush was echoed by non-partisan sources all year. We noted 152 instances when reporters drew into question or refuted campaign statements. More than half (52%) of these corrections targeted the Bush campaign; the remaining 48% were divided evenly between the Clinton and Perot camps." In other words, more than twice as many Bush statements were refuted by reporters as were Clinton statements.

An analysis of the covers of the most popular news magazines also reveals a clear bias. Combining the totals for *Time*, *Newsweek*, and *U.S. News & World Report* for all of 1992, Clinton made the cover fifteen times to Bush's six. Moreover, Bush's cover photo and/or headline were negative five of the six times and neutral the other, while Clinton's image was positive thirteen of fifteen appearances. Hillary Clinton made the covers three times, two of them positive, while Vice-President Dan Quayle never made it. In all, the Democratic ticket was shown 300 percent more than the Republican ticket, and it got fifteen positive images while the Republicans got none. But, the Republicans did get five times the negative images.

Even the late-night comedians did their share. From the beginning of the year to the election in November, David Letterman, Jay Leno, and Arsenio Hall told 556 jokes about Bush and only 296 about Clinton, despite the fertile soil of Clinton's scandals. During the general election, these three told 161 Bush jokes and only sixty-six Clinton jokes.

Beyond the Facts and Figures

Even general logistical decisions by the media seemed to benefit Clinton. Tom Rosensteil, in his book *Strange Bedfellows*, gives three examples of this.

First, the networks made a conscious decision to focus on the voters rather than on daily campaign events. This approach, of course, helped Clinton by emphasizing those areas in which voters were unhappy.

Second, ABC's series "American Agenda" focused on the campaign every day for the six weeks prior to the election. This was campaign coverage the way most people want it to be, but the network's decision to cover only domestic issues led to what Rosensteil calls:

> a natural advantage for Clinton. All the pieces concerned domestic policy, Clinton's strength. Clinton always had more policy proposals on the table than Bush—a function of his progovernment rather than promarketplace approach. Finally, while Bush's rhetoric could always be balanced [in the news story] against his record, Clinton's could not.

Third, even an ABC producer acknowledged that the network's reduced coverage of the conventions benefited the Democrats greatly. "By truncating the coverage," he said, "you never got to see all the diverse elements of the Democratic party which would scare the sh—— out of the electorate." The truncated coverage also prevented people from seeing the wide variety of speakers at the Republican National Convention: women, blacks, Hispanics, and Asians, all coming together under what the media insisted was not a "big tent."

The Media Research Center keeps track of the "revolving door" between government and the media. The number of liberals and Democrats with such potential conflicts of interest generally outnumbers the conservatives and Republicans by about four-to-one. In the September issue of *Media Watch*, the MRC gives two of many examples from the 1992 campaign. Anne Edwards, formerly of the Mondale-Ferraro campaign, went to the Democratic National Convention to cover it for National Public Radio. By the time the convention was over, she was a member of the Clinton-Gore campaign advance staff. MIT economist Paul Krugman, a contributing editor for *U.S. News and World Report*, was writing for the magazine and simultaneously helping to develop Clinton's economic plan. In several cases, he argued for aspects of Clinton's plan in his columns. Finally, in August, the magazine severed its relationship with Krugman.

The Media Spins the News

The phrase "spin doctor" has earned a solid place in the vocabulary of American politics over the past few years. It refers to those campaign operatives whose job it is to convince reporters to place a certain spin on a story. We expect partisan political operatives to do all they can to slant the news a certain way. What we don't expect is for news correspondents to act as spin doctors in the course of reporting stories.

CBS's Susan Spencer on 20 January: "President Bush has used the word 'free fall' in talking about the economy. 'Free fall' may apply to his popularity as well."

Lisa Myers on the "NBC Nightly News" on 28 January: "It's tough to lead when you don't know where you want to go. Call it a vision; George Bush doesn't seem to have one."

Michael Kramer in the 11 May issue of *Time*: "It would help, too, if the man who sanctioned the infamous Willie Horton ad during his 1988 run for the White House would admit his complicity in developing the images and code words that encourage whites to demonize blacks."

Bryant Gumbel to Clinton campaign member on the 10 August "Today" show: "Are Democrats willing, even anxious, to be as nasty as the president is going to be?"

Michael Duffy, in the 24 August issue of *Time*: "Ever since the Clarence Thomas hearings last fall, the Republican party has been struggling to overcome the perception that its regard for women is only a notch or two higher than that of the Navy Tailhook Association."

Joe Klein in *Newsweek*, 31 August: "The whole week was double-ply, wall-to-wall ugly. . . . The Republican party reached an unimaginably slouchy, and brazen, and constant, level of mendacity last week. . . . He [Bush] is in campaign mode now, which means mendacity doesn't matter, aggression is all and wall-to-wall ugly is the order of battle for the duration."

Ed Bradley on CBS's "60 Minutes" on 4 October: "Throughout the eighties, we heard it over and over–the government doesn't give a d— about people with AIDS. They'd just as soon let them die as lift a finger to help them. Well, that's changing."

Bryant Gumbel to John Chancellor on NBC's "Today" show on 9 October: "What are your expectations? How nasty do you expect George Bush to be?"

ABC's Brit Hume on 12 October: "He [Bush] has succeeded so far in solidifying his position–ten or fifteen points behind."

Liberals Admit Media Bias

Even liberal journalists could not deny the clear bias of the media. Sidney Stark, writing in the liberal *Boston Globe*, said as early as 16 March:

> Many reporters may truly believe a Clinton victory is essential for the good of the country. Still, the question is whether the coverage, as a whole, has become so one-sided that the mainstream press is not giving the public the whole truth. That has clearly happened.

Mickey Kaus of the liberal *New Republic* said on 23 August on C-SPAN, "The media are already incredibly pro-Clinton. I get embarrassed watching the news these days. Every story is twisted against Bush."

James Kedbetter, media critic for the liberal *Village Voice*, had this to say about *Newsweek*'s senior editor Joe Klein: "Clinton has intoxicated an entire subclass of reporters led by Joe Klein. . . . Klein did spin control for Clinton among reporters in New Hampshire, telling anyone who would listen that Clinton was 'the smartest politician I've ever met.'"

On "Inside Washington" on 15 August, Evan Thomas, *Newsweek* Washington bureau chief, said, "The Republicans are going to whack away at the press for the next couple of months as being pro-Clinton. And you know what? They're right. The press is pro-Clinton—not 80-20, but I think at least 60-40. There are a lot of formerly liberal reporters out there who would like to see the Democrats win."

Liberal columnist Morton Kondracke admitted to the Media Research Center, "I think that at a certain point, the media stopped doing the investigative job on Bill Clinton that it started. The Republicans are complaining about it, and I think, to a certain extent, they have a right to. I think some of my colleagues have been cheering Clinton. When Clinton . . . went on his bus trip, [they] were completely losing their objectivity. They went bananas for Clinton-Gore. They've hopped aboard the bandwagon, and I just hope they hop off."

Time writer William A. Henry III during election-night coverage on PBS: "We're unpopular because the press tends to be liberal, and I don't think we can run away from that. And I think we're unpopular with a lot of conservatives and Republicans this time because the White House press corps by and large detested

George Bush, probably for good and sufficient reason. They certainly can cite chapter and verse. But their real contempt for him showed through in their reporting in a way that I think got up the nose of the American people."

Former *Newsweek* reporter Jacob Weisberg in the 23 November issue of the liberal *New Republic*: "Indeed, coverage of the campaign vindicated exactly what conservatives have been saying for years about liberal bias in the media. In their defense, journalists say that though they may have their personal opinions, as professionals they are able to correct for them when they write. Sounds nice, but I'm not buying any."

Jon Katz, executive producer of the "CBS Morning News," said on 11 October, "It is the national press corps' dirty little secret that many reporters are out-of-synch with much of America, talking to pollsters and spokesmen more than people, sympathetic to Democratic causes and issues, clinging to the ridiculous and transparently false premise that they are objective and without agendas of their own."

An Unspoken Conspiracy

There was no need for reporters and producers to meet furtively in smoke-filled rooms to plan the overthrow of George Bush. There was already a consensus among reporters that it was time for Bush to go, and, by the early months of 1992, there was a consensus that Clinton was the man who could beat him. In the end, the actions of the media were not much different than they would have been had there been a real conspiracy afoot.

It may well be, of course, that it was time for a change in America's leadership. Twelve years is a long time for either party to stay in the White House, and George Bush certainly did seem to lack vision. But, that is for the people to decide, not the media. A democracy, by definition, demands an informed public. If the information given to the public is slanted or distorted, then the people's votes will not lead to the public policy decisions they desire. In this book you will see that, in the 1992 presidential election campaign, the American public was consciously and consistently misinformed.

Chapter Two

Giving Us the Willies

Everyone remembers the Willie Horton television commercial from the 1988 campaign. Or do they? How many people know that there were two "Willie Horton" ads, that only one actually showed a picture of Willie Horton, and that the one showing Horton aired only on cable channels? Furthermore, how many people know that that particular ad was not produced by the Republican party or funded with campaign funds?

Willie Horton, of course, is the convicted murderer who, out on weekend parole under a program sponsored by Massachusetts governor Michael Dukakis, kidnapped a Maryland couple, stabbed the man and raped the woman. The incident was a perfect illustration of Bush's claim that Dukakis was "soft on crime." So, the decision was made to produce a commercial attacking the controversial furlough program.

The commercial produced by the Republican party is quite tame. In slow motion black and white, a line of prisoners file into and out of a revolving iron door, while an announcer talks about the furlough program. There is no mention of Willie Horton. A majority of the prisoners shown are white or Hispanic, a conscious decision made by the producers. There is, quite simply, nothing racist or even controversial about the commercial.

But, prior to this commercial, Floyd Brown of the Presidential Victory Committee, a conservative organization with no official ties to the Republican party or the Bush campaign, had produced a commercial of his own. It went like this:

(*Photos of Bush and Dukakis over words, "Bush and Dukakis on crime."*)

Narrator: Bush and Dukakis on crime.

(*Photo of Bush over words "Supports Death Penalty."*)

Narrator: Bush supports the death penalty for first-degree murderers.

(*Photo of Dukakis over words "Opposes Death Penalty," then the words "Allowed Murderers to Have Weekend Passes."*)

Narrator: Dukakis not only opposes the death penalty, he allowed first-degree murderers to have weekend passes from prison.

(*Police photo of Willie Horton over his name.*)

Narrator: One was Willie Horton, who murdered a boy in a robbery, stabbing him 19 times.

(*Photo of Horton being put into a police van over words "Horton Received 10 Weekend Passes from Prison."*)

Narrator: Despite a life sentence, Horton received 10 weekend passes from prison.

(*Words change to "Kidnapping, Stabbing, Raping."*)

Narrator: Horton fled, kidnapped a young couple, stabbing the man and repeatedly raping his girlfriend.

(*Photo of Dukakis over words "Weekend Prison Passes. Dukakis on Crime."*)

Narrator: Weekend prison passes. Dukakis on crime.

This commercial was widely denounced as "racist." But, go back and read the transcript again. You'll notice that race is never mentioned. Is the ad racist because it shows a criminal who is a black man? Would the same ad have been racist had the criminal been white? How could that be?

The Media's Reaction

During the 1988 campaign, the media said repeatedly that the Willie Horton ad was "racist" and that George Bush was "introducing sleaze" into the campaign. *Newsweek* said that the Horton "campaign" was based on "code words" and "thinly veiled messages" designed to appeal to "white fear." Bryant Gumbel, in a 2 November 1988 interview with Bush, asked, "Can you deny that the Willie Horton ad tapped a rather rich vein of American racism?" But, again, Bush had nothing to do with the Willie Horton ad, and the ad produced by his campaign tapped society's fear of crime, not its fear of any particular race.

Crime is a legitimate issue, and the Massachusetts furlough program was a legitimate target. As Jeffrey Hart said, "Yes, Willie Horton is black. The ad was valid, and would have been just as valid if the murderer Horton had been green or blue." Hart went on to point out that the liberal media seldom gets excited about negative ads by the Democrats, such as Lyndon Johnson's infamous 1964 commercial that suggested that Barry Goldwater would lead the country into a nuclear war.

Not only were the media's accusations inaccurate, they actually backfired. Because so few people saw the true Willie Horton ad, almost no one knew that Horton was black until the media repeatedly told them he was. "The ad was called racist on the grounds that it's about a black man raping a white woman," Floyd Brown says. "But the ad doesn't reveal the race of the victims. That wasn't in the ad; that was only in the coverage." To whatever degree racist fears played a part in the success of the Bush charges about Dukakis's stance on crime, it is thanks to the media.

The Gore Connection

The media consistently failed to remember that Willie Horton and the prison furlough issue had first been raised by Al Gore when he was battling Dukakis in the 1988 primaries. After he was selected as Clinton's running mate in 1992, he was asked about this on "This Week with David Brinkley." He acknowledged raising the issue of the prison furlough system but insisted that "I didn't know [Willie Horton's] name, much less what his race was." But, the furlough system was first exposed by the Lawrence, Massachusetts *Eagle Tribune* in a series of reports that had focused on Willie Horton. This series came out during the primaries and is the only possible source for the Gore campaign at that time. It is highly unlikely that Gore knew nothing about Horton. Either way, if Bush's discussion of the furlough system was "racist," he was only borrowing a cue from Gore.

In 1990, Thomas Edsall of the *Washington Post* said that Gore had "raised the issue of Willie Horton" during the 1988 primaries. But, during the 1992 elections, Edsall switched to the accepted story that Lee Atwater and the Bush campaign had created the Horton campaign.

Characterizing George Bush: CBS

By 1992, the media had used the Willie Horton ad as its main weapon to suggest that George Bush always fought dirty in his campaigns–a characterization that simply wasn't true. His claims about Michael Dukakis–that he was soft on crime, soft on the military, and a "card-carrying" liberal–had all been true, and each of them dealt directly with how Dukakis would run the country if elected. The media persisted in labeling Bush with terms such as "sleaze," "smear tactics," and "dirty tricks." They also persisted in connecting him to the real Willie Horton ad, as in this report of 30 March on the "CBS Evening News":

> **Dan Rather:** Get ready for more negative advertising in the presidential campaign. The whole campaign may be about to get a lot dirtier. The man behind the ad that helped destroy Michael Dukakis in 1988 said today he's preparing a new assault on Bill Clinton. Bill Plante is at the White House.
>
> (*Television screen on which the real Willie Horton ad is running.*)
>
> **Plante:** If you liked the 1988 presidential campaign, you're going to love 1992.
>
> **Ad Narrator:** Dukakis not only opposes the death penalty, he allowed first degree murderers to have weekend passes. One was Willie Horton.
>
> **Plante:** Brown . . . says there is no connection with the Bush campaign. The White House was alarmed enough to send an assistant press secretary door-to-door in the press room today to disavow Brown's committee and demand that he stop soliciting funds. They may be a little sensitive in the White House because of what

happened in 1988. One man who worked on the Horton ad was working at the same time for the official Bush campaign. The producer of the Horton spot had previously worked for Bush media advisor Roger Ailes. And this time around, Democrats don't buy the idea that there's no connection.

Wendy Sherman, Former Dukakis Campaign Official: I would bet there's not a viewer tonight who believes that this isn't connected to George Bush and his efforts to win reelection.

Plante: Bill Clinton wasn't buying it either.

Clinton: George Bush said on "David Frost" that he would do anything it took to win. I'm getting sick and tired of people who are too weak-kneed to take him on.

Plante: In case there's any doubt about what kind of campaign lies ahead, a senior official said today that the President will make family values a key campaign issue, but that he won't be doing any ads attacking Bill Clinton's character. "No," said the official, "the President will let others do that."

Notice that the report includes no comment from Bush or anyone on his staff, only comments from Democrats specifically accusing the president of the United States of lying. No evidence is offered to support these allegations. Even the 1988 ad is smeared with guilt by association: The producer of the Horton spot had "previously worked for" someone who worked for Bush.

In short, the media used the Willie Horton ad to help create the impression that the Republicans were guilty of negative and unethical campaigning. They continued this little smear campaign on a regular basis.

NBC's Andrea Mitchell, appearing on the "Today" show on 21 October 1991, explained why Clarence Thomas had been appointed to the Supreme Court despite Anita Hill's allegations: "It's the same thing that happened in the 1988 campaign. The Republicans know how to fight dirty." Anita Hill's allegations had become public through an unauthorized leak which violated a promise to Hill that her anonymity would be maintained. The Senate Judiciary Committee, predominantly Democratic, had already examined the allegations and dismissed them as unsubstantiated. Their leakage to the liberal National Public Radio was clearly a partisan attempt to derail Thomas's confirmation by introducing sleaze into the hearings. And, it was the Republicans who had fought dirty?

Giving Us the Willies

In fact, by 1992 the media had misrepresented the Willie Horton ad so successfully and so consistently that it became a generic term for any campaign strategy that was, in the eyes of the media, negative, even when such strategies concerned legitimate issues.

CNN's David French, in his commentary of 21 May, was discussing Dan Quayle's comment about the "Murphy Brown" television show. Showing Bush's revolving door ad, French intoned, "In the same way Willie Horton symbolized the crime issue in the '88 campaign, 'Murphy Brown' has entered the Republican issues Hall of Fame on this year's theme of family values." (This was just one of many instances where Bush's ad was identified as a Willie Horton ad.)

Deborah Tannen, in a 12 October *New York Times* essay, said, "It is reassuring that the Republican attempts to make Bill Clinton's wife into 'Willary Horton' failed. . . ."

During the Republican convention, Andrea Mitchell on the PBS/NBC combined coverage, said that the

Democrats claim the Republicans are using family values "as a wedge issue and that this is going to be the Willie Horton issue of this campaign."

Katie Couric, interviewing Pat Buchanan on the "Today" show on 6 May, asked, "Many are afraid the L.A. riots are going to be the Willie Horton of this campaign. Are you afraid they're going to have a divisive effect? Does that concern you or are you playing that up?"

Eric Engberg, evaluating campaign rhetoric on the "CBS Evening News" on 23 September, began with a sound bite of George Bush saying, "Governor Clinton still has not brought a civil rights bill to the people of Arkansas." "It is true," says Engberg, "that Arkansas and Alabama are the only two states without a civil rights law. But time out. George Bush's civil rights record is less than pristine. He vetoed the civil rights bill of 1990 and when he ran for the Senate in '64 he campaigned against the Civil Rights Act. He built his '88 campaign around the Willie Horton issue."

Liberal Censorship

All of which is bad enough. But, then the media went so far as to censor the renewed efforts of Floyd Brown at the request of the Democratic party.

After the revelations of Gennifer Flowers, Brown set up a toll-free number people could call to hear outtakes of the Flowers-Clinton tapes. After all, unlike the Watergate tapes, not a single national news show or magazine had published outtakes or transcripts of the tapes. But, when Brown tried to air a commercial advertising the toll-free number, he ran into a brick wall. Time Warner, a major sponsor of the Democratic National Convention, refused to air the commercial on a cable channel in New York. Then, Democratic party chairman Ron Brown sent letters to 1,500 cable systems and television stations intimidating them into refusing the commercials.

The letter, written on Democratic National Committee letterhead, began:

> Dear Station Manager, I am writing you on a matter of great concern to me and, I am sure, to the vast majority of the American people who want to see this year's Presidential election determined on the issues rather than by the smear tactics which have characterized so many recent elections and have denigrated our political process.

Brown describes Floyd Brown's commercial, claims that the tapes "have been deliberately altered in such a way as to substantially distort them," and talks about the "shocking reports" on CBS about Floyd Brown's attempts to investigate allegations of another affair:

> The disgust over Floyd Brown's tactics has cut across the political spectrum. After the first CBS broadcast ran, the White House said that President Bush was "very upset" about the report, and the President himself stated that he would do whatever he could to stop Floyd Brown from using his name for such "nefarious purposes. . . ."
>
> Under these circumstances, I think it is fair to say that by airing ads produced by Floyd Brown and his associates, your station would contribute to the enhancement and promotion of smear campaigns of the vilest type. In addition, American voters stand to suffer if such ads are aired and their focus is turned from the issues to such sleaze.
>
> These types of tactics are not new for Floyd Brown and those working for him. The organi-

> zation with which he was associated in 1988 was the group that produced the infamous Willie Horton ads. . . .
>
> Floyd Brown is likely to continue his sleaze campaign, and there is no reason why this time his type of scurrilous advertising should see the light of day. In the first place, I am advised that under FCC rules, your station has no obligation whatsoever to run such ads. I am also advised that if you were to run the ads, you may well incur an obligation to run responses on behalf of Governor Clinton. You should also be aware that the ads may well violate the privacy and other rights of other affected persons, such as the family recently hounded by Floyd Brown.
>
> I trust you will agree that our country deserves better in this election than being subjected to another "Willie Horton" campaign, and please accept my personal thanks for whatever you can do to ensure that this does not reoccur.

The letter is signed "Ronald H. Brown, Chairman, Democratic National Committee."

This is an extraordinary letter. Even if one agrees that Floyd Brown's tactics have no place in a presidential campaign, it is simply astounding that the chairman of a major political party could ask the free press of America to censor the campaign advertisements of its opponents without causing an uproar of indignation. Think of the media's response had this letter, complete with its veiled threats of legal action, been signed by a Republican like Lee Atwater, John Sununu, or James Baker. The same media that was disgusted by a single sentence from Dan Quayle about a television show saw no reason to get excited about this blatant attempt to suppress information. On the contrary, television stations and cable systems across the country cooperated with the Democratic party, and Floyd Brown's commercial ran in only a few places.

Such censorship is not unusual. In the same election, voters in Colorado were to vote on Amendment 2, which would prohibit the granting of minority status to homosexuals. All three Denver television stations refused to run proamendment commercials. Across the country, prolife candidates were not allowed to run anti-abortion commercials on the grounds that they were "too explicit." In this book, you will learn of several other examples of such censorship. All of these censored commercials have only one thing in common: they are produced by conservatives.

A strange contradiction: the Democratic party and the media are predominantly liberal, and liberals oppose censorship. Yet, in this blatant incident, there was nary a whimper in defense of Floyd Brown.

Chapter Three

The Affairs of State

By the end of January, Bill Clinton had emerged as the Democratic front-runner in the New Hampshire primary. But, on Thursday, 23 January, a bombshell hit–a blonde bombshell named Gennifer Flowers. The former beauty queen and lounge singer–now a state government employee–had sold her story of a twelve-year affair with Governor Clinton to the supermarket tabloid called the *Star*. She claimed she could back her story up with a taped telephone conversation in which Clinton assured her that no one could prove anything. Advanced copies of the story were given to the mainstream media, who immediately confronted Clinton on the allegations.

Clinton, on camera, denied the charges. His calm, even smiling, demeanor suggested that he was perhaps telling the truth. In reality, his poise was partially the result of the fact that a producer at ABC had leaked the allegations to the campaign, giving Clinton time both to brace himself emotionally and to prepare an answer.

The Media Response

On Thursday, 23 January, the day the media was informed of the allegations, NBC gave Clinton an almost completely positive "Decision 92" profile in the second half of the newscast. Tom Brokaw's lead-in included a comment about the allegations but did not mention Gennifer Flower's name. In fact, Brokaw added that Clinton produced a year-old letter from Flowers' lawyer in which the lawyer denies the allegations of an affair on Flowers' behalf. The allegations were mentioned by correspondent Lisa Myers deep in the profile but, again, without any details. The next day, NBC's "Today" show covered the story briefly but, again, without giving details. The "Nightly News" failed to mention it that night or the next. It was mentioned briefly on Sunday evening toward the end of the newscast.

PBS's "MacNeil/Lehrer Newshour" skipped the story; the justification being that the story was "unsubstantiated."

CBS gave the story more coverage. It was the third story on Friday night, 24 January, the lead story on Saturday and Monday, and was mentioned in Tuesday's newscast. On Sunday night, of course, CBS broadcast the famous "60 Minutes" interview. One cannot help wonder if CBS's dedication to the story had anything to do with the fact that it served as a promo for one of their shows.

The *New York Times*, on the day the media was first notified, ran only a tiny story on page 7 containing Clinton's denial. The *Washington Post* ran a story on page 10 that focused on how the media was handling the allegations.

The day after Clinton appeared with his wife on "60 Minutes," Gennifer Flowers held her famous press conference. Local affiliates ran with it on their eleven o'clock broadcasts, and CNN started carrying it, virtually forcing the rest of the national media to cover it at last.

So that morning, 27 January, "Today" led with the story, as it would the next day. That night, "Nightly News" covered it for the first and last time, but only after a scintillating story about disagreements over loans between the United States and Israel. The next night, it was mentioned only in a John Chancellor commentary saying that the issue should now be forgotten. And that was it–NBC's total prime-time coverage of the allegations consisted of two brief mentions late in the newscasts, one full story, and a commentary supporting Clinton.

In all, according to the Media Research Center, the three network evening news shows ran a grand total of fourteen stories on the allegations. Hardly a media feeding frenzy.

It is surprising–and significant–that Flowers was not invited to appear on any of the morning talk shows, nor was she invited to appear on "Larry King Live," "Donahue," or "Oprah."

What is more surprising is that virtually no investigative reporting was conducted in an attempt to discover the truth behind the charges. Remember, this is the same media that prides itself for bringing down Richard Nixon, and in which every reporter dreams of making his mark by uncovering some major scandal. Yet, the investigative powers of this huge industry utterly failed when it came to finding the merest shred of evidence either for or against the Flowers allegations.

Eleanor Clift, writing in the 10 February issue of *Newsweek*, said, "Gary Hart would have given anything for the support Clinton got last week. Truth is, the press is willing to cut Clinton some slack because they like him–and what he has to say. He is a policy wonk in tune with a younger generation of Democrats eager to take the party beyond the liberal stereotype."

Unpaid Media Consultants

Tom Rosensteil, in *Strange Bedfellows,* chronicles two examples of explicit help Clinton received from the media in his moment of crisis. First, Richard N. Kaplan, executive producer for ABC's "Prime Time Live," acted as a behind-the-scenes media consultant for Clinton:

> Kaplan had been a friend of Clinton's for more than a decade. "There is no way to avoid relationships with politicians," Kaplan explained later. "I knew that he was not 'Slick Willie' and not a scourge and really a terrific, terrific person."

Amazingly, Kaplan had managed over the past twelve years not to become friends with either Ronald Reagan or George Bush, whom his show had covered many times. But, there was "no way to avoid" a friendship with a governor one thousand miles away. A judge with the same level of detachment as Kaplan would pull himself off the case. Kaplan, instead, initiated an effort to use his show to help Clinton save himself:

> Kaplan called Clinton advisor Susan Thomases, a mutual friend. "Bill has to come out and do something about this," he told her. Why not his show, *Prime Time Live.* Since it was live, the candidate would have some control. And they should have Hillary on, too, he told Thomases, appearing alongside her husband. . . .
>
> Soon Clinton called Kaplan for advice. . . . "I am really torn. You know her story isn't true," an obviously frightened Clinton said. . . .
>
> "Do the toughest interview you can," Kaplan advised Clinton. If you want to prove your cred-

> ibility, you don't want to do it on *Good Morning America* or the *Today Show*. . . ."

Missing in Kaplan's advice is the question of why the media should help a candidate prove his credibility at all, much less before Kaplan himself knew whether or not the story was true. But, even Kaplan's blatant efforts at advocacy pale beside another event that occurred during the taping of the famous "60 Minutes" interview with Bill and Hillary.

> *60 Minutes* executive producer Don Hewitt had his own agenda. Twice during the taping he kneeled by Clinton and exhorted the candidate to admit to adultery. He had helped make a president in 1960 as producer of the Nixon-Kennedy debates, he said. He could do it again now. People would love the candor, he was suggesting. They could create a president here, he said.

Hewitt's advice was probably correct—this was one of those rare occasions when the morally right thing would also have been the politically wise thing. What is frightening is Hewitt's obvious belief that there is nothing wrong with those in the media attempting to "make" a president. Doesn't that fly in the face of the media's constant grumbling about politicians manipulating the press? And, what does Hewitt mean that he helped "make" a president before—did he do something as producer of the Nixon-Kennedy debates that affected the outcome?

When Nixon was caught lying over the Watergate scandal, had Hewitt knelt at his side and exhorted him to save his presidency by admitting the truth and asking forgiveness? When Reagan and Bush were suspected of lying about the Iran-Contra affair, had Hewitt rushed to them with his advice?

The Tapes

At her press conference, Gennifer Flowers distributed a transcript of taped telephone conversations with Bill Clinton. The media was quick to assert that the tapes did not prove an affair had occurred, but they did not let their readers decide for themselves. NBC played only one short excerpt only one time, and the reporter did not follow up on the fact that Clinton was clearly heard to lie in that excerpt. The Associated Press quoted only twenty-four words from the tapes, and the *Washington Post* quoted only fifty-nine. (That paper had taken the Nixon tapes a bit more seriously.) *Time, Newsweek,* and *U.S. News and World Report* all failed to quote a single word.

There is some truth to the assertion that the tapes fail to confirm an affair between Clinton and Flowers. Unlike the media, however, we will let our readers decide for themselves. You will find the complete transcript of the tapes in Appendix A.

Some media outlets questioned the authenticity of the tapes. But, Clinton, amazingly, acknowledged their authenticity when he apologized to Mario Cuomo for ethnic comments he made on those tapes. Yet, still the media ignored them. Todd Gitlin of the *Washington Journalism Review* even referred to it as a "purported telephone conversation."

If the tapes do not prove anything, why was a campaign begun by the Clinton camp to discredit them? Clinton spokesperson Mandy Grunwald said on ABC's *Viewpoint,* "Those tapes, as I think everybody knows, were edited and edited and edited. . . ." Not surprisingly, the media picked up on this claim. *Newsweek* said the tapes were "doctored," although it offered no proof of this. The magazine accepted Clinton's explanation that he had talked to Flowers only to calm her down because she was distraught over rumors of an affair between them. But, wasn't Flowers the one who subsequently made the affair public in a called press conference and a front-page story in a tabloid for which she was paid?

"Bimbo Eruptions"

On 26 July, the *Washington Post* ran a story about Jack Palladino, a $2,000-a-day private investigator hired by the Clinton campaign to handle what campaign official Betsy Wright called "bimbo eruptions." Palladino's job was to dig up dirt on the women to keep them from going public with their allegations. He had his work cut out for him—by August, well over twenty women had come forward with allegations of dalliance with Clinton. The media could not claim not to know about this. In the 26 July story, Betsy Wright said that there had been nineteen bimbo eruptions since the nomination and seven others earlier, including Flowers.

One such woman was Sally Perdue, a former Miss Arkansas, who appeared on "Sally Jesse Raphael" to tell about a 1983 affair with the governor. Clinton would come to her home in the state limousine, she said, and when they had had their fun, Clinton would flick her porch light to summon his driver. Not only was Ms. Perdue ignored by the rest of the media, the "Sally Jesse Raphael" show on which she appeared was blacked out in New York by WABC-TV, an affiliate wholly owned by ABC. Oddly, this blatant example of censorship was not protested by the usual First Amendment purists.

The *Post* article on private investigator Jack Palladino said that he had called "former associates and estranged relatives" of Ms. Perdue "seeking damaging comments about her credibility." He asked one such person if she would talk to reporters about Perdue. No other publication took issue with the use of a private investigator paid with campaign donations, even though they had viciously attacked Ross Perot for his use of private investigators paid from his own pocket.

A week after the *Post* story appeared, none of the networks had picked up the story. But, when Mary Matalin, Bush's deputy campaign manager, issued a press release pointing out the impropriety of using "thousands of taxpayer dollars on private investigators to fend off bimbo eruptions," all four news networks accused the Bush campaign of introducing "sleaze" into the campaign. The press release "broke the President's personal promise to avoid sleaze," said CBS White House correspondent Susan Spencer. ABC's Forrest Sawyer called it "mudslinging." CBS's Connie Chung introduced the story by saying, "There is new evidence that the Bush reelection campaign is out of control." Only ABC's Brit Hume pointed out that the term "bimbo eruptions" came from the Clinton campaign. Not a single one of the news shows pointed out that the charge in Matalin's press release was entirely true.

The *New York Times* denounced the "bimbo eruptions" phrase without revealing its origins. The *Boston Globe*, in an editorial, said, "There is no Willie Horton in sight this year, so the Bush campaign team has come up with 'bimbo eruptions'—whatever they may be."

The Case of Susann Coleman

Soon after this, an anonymous letter was sent to news organizations claiming that, fifteen years before, a woman named Susann Coleman had killed herself following an affair with Clinton that had left her pregnant. Floyd Brown, the independent Republican operative who had produced the real Willie Horton ad, engaged private detectives to check out the story. When he was unable to confirm the story, he dropped it.

But when CBS learned of Brown's efforts, they ran it as the lead story on 14 July. In marked contrast to the Clinton campaign, the use of private investigators suddenly became, in the words of correspondent Eric Engberg, "police state tactics." Floyd Brown points out the contradiction in CBS's approach. "Floyd Brown researches it, CBS researches it," he said. "Floyd Brown finds no validity to the story and drops it. . . . CBS finds no validity to the story and puts it into millions of homes. I would say CBS has been very irresponsible." In other words, CBS did not mind besmirching Susann Coleman's name if doing so would help them besmirch the Republicans, as well.

In his story, Engberg referred to the letter as nothing more than "a nasty hoax." CBS could know this only if it had also investigated the story as Brown had done. And who had first brought the story to CBS's attention? Jack Palladino.

The Case of Charlette Perry

The main defense given by the media for not focusing on the Flowers allegations was that a candidate's private life should not enter into the campaign so long as it doesn't affect his performance in office. Then a revelation was made that destroyed that defense.

Charlette Perry, a black woman, was a secretary in the Arkansas state government. In 1991, she was recommended for a promotion to supervisor of the secretarial pool, a promotion she clearly deserved. Because of the agency's policy of hiring from within, the promotion was practically assured.

Then, something went wrong. Ms. Perry was informed that the job description suddenly had been rewritten to require public relations skills and knowledge of computers, neither of which were really essential to the job and neither of which Ms. Perry had. The job instead went to an attractive white woman who had not previously worked in that or any other state agency. Her name: Gennifer Flowers.

Ms. Perry filed a complaint, and a grievance committee found that the position should have been filled from within the agency. The committee's report went to the head of the agency, Don K. Barnes, a Clinton appointee, who rejected the findings without stating a reason.

The story was reported by the print and electronic media in Little Rock well after Bill Clinton became a presidential candidate, and the grievance committee findings are a matter of public record. In addition, the Flowers-Clinton tapes contain a discussion of the matter. When Flowers asks Clinton what she should do if reporters ask her about the matter, Clinton says, "If they ever ask if you've talked to me about it, you can just say no."

With such evidence, it would take a concerted effort to avoid breaking this story nationally. Nevertheless, not a single major media outlet carried the story. Even when *Newsday* did a 3,600-word story on it, everyone else managed to avoid mentioning it.

On 16 September, Reed Irvine, director of Accuracy In Media, Inc., took part in a discussion on media bias in the campaign. The discussion, held at Rice University, was broadcast as an ABC "Viewpoint" special on late night. Roone Arledge, president of ABC News and John Stacks, deputy managing editor of *Time*, were asked by Irvine why the Charlette Perry story had not broken. Roone Arledge claimed that he knew nothing about the story and pointed out that most people thought the media had already overdone the subject of Gennifer Flowers.

> One of the issues we wrestle with on a regular basis, is to what degree [candidates'] private lives are fair game for the press. . . . We have normally come down on the side that if it affects their work, if it has something to do with the performance of their job, or if the candidate himself responds to these charges, then it becomes news. If this had been an issue that was widely distributed—I don't know where *Newsday* got that story from, or where you got it from, or even if it's true—I'm not saying it isn't true. Perhaps it is. It probably would have been covered in some degree. . . .

Irvine pointed out, of course, that a governor denying a job to a qualified candidate in order to hire his mistress is surely a case which "has something to do with the performance" of his job. Yet, even after being alerted to the story on nationwide television, neither ABC nor *Time* got around to reporting on it. For a liberal media that usually rushes to cover instances in which blacks and women are discriminated against, the press remained surprisingly quiet on this one.

The Character Issue

Following the allegations of draft dodging and marital infidelity, the media began to form a consensus that they would not cover "character issues." Is it coincidence that they would make this decision in the very year that their favorite candidate was threatened by such issues? Just one year before, Clarence Thomas had been skewered on questions about his character, and the media had been all for it. The media continued to be hypocritical about character issues throughout the 1992 campaign.

Five days before the election, Democratic consultant Mark Siegal, on "Crossfire," accused President Bush of lying about Iran-Contra, stating that it suggests a flawed character. But, when Republican Haley Barbour mentioned Gennifer Flowers, Siegal went on a tirade:

> I don't want to talk about Gennifer Flowers. Let's not talk about Gennifer Flowers, okay? . . . And stop attacking the character of the next president of the United States. I resent it. And I resent the big lies that you're throwing around.

Throughout the campaign, Clinton and Gore hit Bush hard about Iran-Contra, repeatedly accusing him of lying. Yet, those in the campaign and those in the media were consistent in denouncing as "sleaze" anyone who wanted to present evidence that Clinton was a liar.

Most hypocritical of all was the dragging up of old rumors of a Bush affair that had long ago been investigated and dismissed. A new book called *The Power House*, by Susan Trento, included a brief statement from a now-deceased former ambassador saying he had arranged for Vice-President George Bush to have time alone with his aide, Jennifer Fitzgerald, during a 1984 visit to Geneva. Surely, this was a less substantiated claim than Gennifer Flowers'. The *Los Angeles Times*, CNN, and even the *Washington Post* examined the story and decided it was too flimsy to run. But, the *New York Post*, a tabloid, ran it on 11 August with the headline "The Bush Affair." In marked contrast to their hesitation about the Gennifer Flowers story, all three networks ran the story that night, and all three morning shows ran lengthy segments. Wire stories on the allegations were widely reprinted.

What's Good for the Goose . . .

The *Washington Post*, on 27 March, published a story by Howard Kurtz entitled "Turning Over Little

Rock to Dig Up Clinton's Past." The subtitle protests that the "Press Has Not Published a Comparable Barrage of Scandal-Type Stories about Bush." Kurtz quotes Jack Nelson, Washington bureau chief for the *Los Angeles Times*, as saying, "There is a tremendous imbalance. I don't see anybody digging over Bush's record. . . ." He also quotes Clinton as saying, "It would be interesting to have an audit of the person-hours devoted to the investigation of my life, my work, my campaign, and compare it to the scrutiny given Bush or the other Democratic candidates." But, as Kurtz himself points out, Bush *was* subjected to intense scrutiny when he first became a candidate in 1980. Besides, Bush had spent his career in national politics as a congressman, an ambassador, and as director of the CIA. He had been well known to the national press corps when he had first become a candidate in the 1980 race, and, by 1992, there was literally nothing new to be said about him.

In fact, Kurtz goes so far as to say, "The pattern is familiar: A newcomer bursts onto the national stage and is quickly subjected to a withering crossfire by the investigative guns of the press. It happened to Rep. Geraldine A. Ferrara (D-N.Y.) in 1984 and to Sen. Dan Quayle (R-Ind.) in 1988." In other words, what was happening to Clinton was what happened to all candidates of both parties.

The other complaint made by the article is that nearly all the stories about Clinton were, in the words of Jack Nelson, merely "recycled from Arkansas." Does this suggest that because a scandal had been widely known in Arkansas for years, that it should therefore *not* be reported to the nation when Clinton enters the national arena? Wasn't Clinton's real problem that there had been so many scandals already widely known?

What we have here is an attempt to make it appear that Clinton is being treated unfairly when the details of the article itself show that he is not. Even the opening, which says that "about 20 reporters" have "descended" on Little Rock, sounds sensational but is, in reality, unimpressive when one considers that there are several hundred major newspapers, four news networks, and dozens of news journals. The real question might be why so few reporters had made the trek to Little Rock.

A similar attempt was made two weeks later by the *New York Times*. "Bush May Get a Closer Look After What Clinton Endured," read the headline to Andrew Rosenthal's story. The story drags up every old rumor, suggesting that they have not been investigated thoroughly enough. But, even Rosenthal admits that Bush *has* undergone a great deal of scrutiny. When he quotes analyst Kevin Phillips saying that there has been no scrutiny of Bush's sons and siblings and their financial dealing, he admits that Phillips underestimates the amount of coverage. If Phillips' statement is incorrect, why does Rosenthal quote it in the first place? How can Phillips be qualified as an expert when he can't even remember the intense scrutiny undergone by Neil Bush in the wake of the S&L scandal? And, what about the integrity of Phillips' call to investigate Bush's "sons and siblings" instead of Bush himself? Clinton's brother had been arrested on cocaine charges, but the media wasn't trying to find additional dirt on him, and few people thought Roger Clinton's problems had any bearing on Clinton's ability to lead.

Todd Gitlin, writing in the *Washington Journalism Review*, also made the claim that Bush had not been treated as harshly as Clinton. Like the others, he used the occasion to bring up the rumors of adultery, and, like the others, he failed to tell us that those claims had indeed been investigated years ago and that no evidence had ever surfaced to substantiate them.

Jack Nelson complained to the *Post* that the coverage of past drug charges against Jerry Brown "smacked of moving ahead with a story without enough facts." But, just two weeks later, on CNN's "Reliable Sources," Nelson agreed with Democratic party chairman Ron Brown that the media should pay more attention to the rumors of Bush's extramarital affair. "What is good for the goose is good for the gander, I guess, and I suppose that maybe Ron Brown has a point that if this is an issue, it should be brought up for both candidates." It must have bothered Nelson that his own paper had been one of the few to give adequate coverage to Clinton's draft issue.

Bob Beckel, Walter Mondale's 1984 campaign manager, sat in as the liberal host on CNN's "Crossfire" one night in April. He chastised Dave Bartlett of the Radio and Television News Directors Association for what he called the most irresponsible performance by the press in twenty years. His complaint? Why, all the "sleaze" that had been covered concerning Bill Clinton. Think of the effect all this has probably had on Clinton's daughter, he said. "They always scream about, 'no issues, no issues, we want to hear about issues,' then they report on the sleaze. It's really a two-faced press corps if ever I saw one."

Beckel should know. Not long before his CNN appearance, he had taken part in a forum broadcast by C-SPAN, where he had urged the media to investigate the rumors that George Bush had had an extramarital affair. They should "find" the woman, he had said (which wouldn't be difficult since she was now a senior official at the State Department). If the media is going to report such things about Clinton, Beckel had said, they should do the same for Bush. This had prompted Eric Engberg of CBS News to point out that Gennifer Flowers had come forward of her own account and had provided audio tapes of her conversations with Clinton. Not only had no woman come forward to admit an affair with Bush, but no third party had ever made efforts to make public such a claim.

As Engberg suggests, all those who took it on themselves to try to make the media tougher on Bush because of Clinton's misfortunes miss several points. First, Clinton's scandals were not the result of investigative reporting by the media. Both the Gennifer Flowers allegations and the draft allegations were handed to the media, and few details were added to either story as the result of media efforts. Second, the idea that Bush should have as much bad press as Clinton presumes that Bush has done as many bad things as Clinton, a presumption that must necessarily prevent objectivity in reporting. The media seems to ignore the possibility that Bush simply did not do the same type of things as Clinton had done. The fact that Clinton has been hit harder than Bush suggests not that the media has been biased, but that Clinton does indeed have character problems that Bush does not have. Third, and most important, is in these articles the very media that claimed that character issues were not important were also calling for more investigation into Bush's character.

And, some, like Bob Beckel, didn't know where to stop. On "Crossfire" on 26 August, he referred to Gennifer Flowers' allegations as "the flimsiest of stories" and said that her claims were "brought to you by the Republican party." He offered no proof of this latter charge.

Chapter Four

Caught in a Draft

The facts of the case are simple and, at this point, indisputable. Bill Clinton was graduated from college in 1968, during the heat of the Vietnam War. In March 1968, he was classified 1-A, meaning that he was ripe for being drafted immediately, providing he passed his physical. But, for some reason he was not ordered to take his physical for over ten months, by which time he was at Oxford on a Rhodes scholarship.

He finally received a draft notice in April 1969, but he somehow succeeded in getting his draft board to put off his induction date until 28 July. When asked by reporters why there was such a long delay, Clinton stated repeatedly that it was merely a fluke and that he had received no special treatment. Within a month or two, thanks to the investigative diligence of the *Los Angeles Times*, it was proven that Clinton had boldly and repeatedly lied.

Here's what really happened: Clinton's uncle, Raymond Clinton, had initiated a diligent effort to protect him from the draft. Henry Britt, attorney to the late Raymond Clinton, told the *Times* that Uncle Raymond had gotten the director of the local Navy Reserve unit to create a vacancy for Clinton, which would allow him to serve two years in the Reserve and free him from the draft. Uncle Raymond then asked the draft board to delay Clinton's notice until he had time to join the Reserve. But, when the time came to join the Reserve, Clinton, now at Oxford, turned down the offer. Britt told the *Times* that the real motive behind the effort was to get Clinton into Oxford.

This only delayed things. When the draft induction came in April 1969, Uncle Raymond and Clinton appealed to Arkansas senator William Fulbright, for whom Clinton had worked when he was a student at Georgetown University. Fulbright asked the ROTC director at the University of Arkansas to state that Clinton was enrolled in ROTC and thus qualified for a deferment. This was illegal in two ways: first, because Clinton was not even enrolled in the school at the time, and, second, because deferments cannot be granted for circumstances arising after an induction notice has been issued.

Meanwhile, a friend and classmate of Clinton, Cliff Jackson, succeeded in getting Arkansas governor Winthrop Rockefeller and Col. Lefty Hawkins, the head of the state Selective Service system, to join in the effort to secure the deferment.

In September, President Nixon announced that graduate students would be allowed to complete the school year. In October, Clinton had his draft classification changed back to 1-A. On 1 December, Clinton drew a number in the draft lottery high enough to ensure his safety. Three days later he reneged on his promise to enroll in the ROTC program, just as he had done with the Reserve. Clinton repeatedly told the media that he decided not to join the ROTC before he knew about his high draft number, but that is refuted by a letter Clinton wrote to ROTC director Col. Eugene Holmes. In that letter, Clinton thanks him for saving him from the draft and describes his loathing of the military.

Clinton's dishonesty to the media on this issue had begun years before. When he first ran for governor in 1978, he told the *Arkansas Gazette* that he never even received the ROTC deferment. Sen. Robert Dole neatly summarized Clinton's latest round of lies to the media: "He says he was never drafted, and he was. Said he never received a deferment, and he did. Said he never opposed the draft, then he finally said he did. He failed to disclose his anti-war activities in an effort to get into the ROTC." And, how well did the media publicize this misinformation?

The Letter

In February, the *Wall Street Journal* quoted Col. Eugene Holmes suggesting Clinton had "manipulated" things in 1969. Major newspapers across the country ran stories the next day, but NBC and CBS decided the story wasn't newsworthy.

The stories that did run prompted the surfacing of a letter Clinton had written—at the age of twenty-three—to Colonel Holmes. The letter is an incredible document, one containing passages that could both help and hurt the candidate. (You will find the letter in its entirety in Appendix B.) Significantly, the letter was dated two days after Clinton had drawn a high draft number. In it, Clinton tried to explain his opposition to the war, "a war I opposed and despised with a depth of feeling I had reserved solely for racism in America before Vietnam. . . ." In addition, he said, he "came to believe that the draft system itself was illegitimate" because the Vietnam conflict "does not involve immediately the peace and freedom of the nation. . . ." These were understandable sentiments and widely shared at the time. While many in the WWII generation would not forgive such feelings, most baby boomers would at least give him credit for the sincerity of his opposition to the war.

But, then the letter goes on to make an astounding confession: "I decided to accept the draft in spite of my beliefs for one reason: to maintain my political viability within the system. For years I have worked to prepare myself for a political life. . . ." Such a comment would strike most people as revealing, at the very least, a calculating and ambitious young man.

Then, to top it off, Clinton goes on to admit that he had used the ROTC to avoid the draft: "After I signed the ROTC letter of intent, I began to wonder whether the compromise I had made with myself was not more objectionable than the draft would have been, because I had no interest in the ROTC program in itself and all I seemed to have done was protect myself from physical harm. . . ." This admission is only slightly balanced by Clinton's earnestness in wishing Colonel Holmes to understand "how so many fine people have come to find themselves still loving their country but loathing the military."

Would the letter help or hurt Clinton? At the very least, it would solidify a mistrust of the candidate following the Flowers affair. But, not to worry; the media succeeded in not only withholding the letter but in letting Clinton turn the whole thing into a victory.

According to Tom Rosensteil, ABC was the first to get a copy of the letter, but Peter Jennings said nothing about it on the evening news. At the same time, a Republican operative named James Tully had secured a copy of the letter, which he gave to former Air Force major general Richard Secord, who in turn gave it to Ted Koppel. Koppel called Clinton's people to invite him onto "Nightline" to talk about the letter, and when he did, he indicated that the "source for the letter had connections to the Pentagon." The savvy Clinton campaigners seized the initiative, called a press conference, and, citing Koppel as their source, claimed that the Pentagon had released the letter to try to hurt Clinton.

The media followed right along. Notice how the "CBS Evening News" report of 12 February is written from the viewpoint of the Clinton campaign:

> **Dan Rather:** In the presidential campaign, Democrat Bill Clinton says Bush-Quayle reelection forces are using a smear campaign to constantly raise questions about his past. And as Richard Threlkeld reports tonight, Clinton had to deal with those questions again today, just six days before the New Hampshire primary.
>
> **Threlkeld:** At a hastily called news conference, Clinton accused the Republicans of trying to wreck his presidential campaign by leaking the contents of a letter he wrote as a young man about his draft status during the Vietnam War.
>
> **Clinton:** We may never know the motives of the people who leaked this letter, but I think it's a fair guess to presume that they did not wish my campaign well, and that they were willing to violate the law to derail it.
>
> **Threlkeld:** For a week now Clinton has been on the stump here claiming that Republicans were behind allegations that he'd had an extramarital affair and that he'd tried to avoid being drafted for Vietnam.
>
> **Clinton:** We know their game plan; they've run against me for years in Arkansas. We've seen it in America before. Divide and destroy before people really get to know the candidate.
>
> **Threlkeld:** Today Clinton produced as evidence a letter he said was leaked to another broadcast network, and Clinton said his aides were told by the network that it was their impression the

letter came from someone at the Pentagon. It was written in 1969 to the head of the university ROTC unit Clinton had then agreed to join but never did. He received a draft deferment as a result but later changed his mind and declared himself eligible, although he was never called up.

(*Two short excerpts of the letter are given.*)

If recent polls are to be believed, Clinton's support here has been hemorrhaging, because of what he insists are Republican dirty tricks played on him because Republicans fear he is the most electable Democrat.

Clinton: It represents a pattern of behavior by people desperate to stay in power, and willing to impugn the motives, the patriotism, and the lives of anyone who stands in their way.

Threlkeld: Both the White House and the Bush campaign deny any involvement in releasing the letter. Clinton, meantime, says he will publish it in tomorrow's newspaper so that New Hampshire voters can decide for themselves.

Clinton's actions are great politics: take the focus off the allegations by making allegations of your own. But, these are also serious charges: Clinton is accusing the president of the United States of breaking federal laws, and he is doing so without proof. There is absolutely no reason to believe the Bush campaign had anything to do with the Gennifer Flowers allegations. The only evidence Clinton offered concerning the letter was that someone at the network thought the letter came from someone at the Pentagon, a situation which wasn't true and which would not have linked the letter to the Bush campaign even if it had been.

Normally, in such a situation, the media would have pursued the charges leveled at Bush, or they would have hammered at Clinton to produce proof or retract the charges. Instead, it merely offered Clinton a bully pulpit for making untrue and unsubstantiated charges. The same reporters who did not accept tape recordings of Clinton himself as proof of Gennifer Flowers's allegations now allowed their candidate to make much more serious charges with far less proof.

When Clinton appeared on "Nightline," Ted Koppel took the unusual step of reading the entire letter on the air. Also unusual was the fact that Clinton appeared alone on the show, with no dissenting voices. He was asked a few nonthreatening questions and given plenty of time to put his own spin on the issue. "In this case," writes Rosensteil, "Koppel helped end the media feeding frenzy at just the moment when the press could have ended Clinton's candidacy."

Political Pull

Senator Fulbright's involvement was disclosed in March by the *Arkansas Democrat* and the *New York Post*, both of which reproduced a memo written by a Fulbright aide. In April, Cliff Jackson revealed his involvement in securing this influence. On 5 April, the *Los Angeles Times* quoted a Jackson letter of 27 August 1969 which said, "Bill Clinton is still trying to wiggle his way out of . . . Arkansas law school. His latest scheme: Because his ROTC training won't start until next year, he is going to ask the ROTC commander to give him special permission to go one more year to Oxford." The national media ignored these revelations. In fact, the *Washington Post* index for the entire three months of April-June shows only five references to draft dodging.

Six months later, on 2 September, the *Los Angeles Times* published a confirmation of Fulbright's influence by Robert Corrado, the last surviving member of Clinton's draft board. The *Times* also published a memo from Col. Eugene Holmes, the University of Arkansas ROTC director, in which he described the pressure applied to him by Fulbright. The story included the fact that Clinton's uncle, Raymond Clinton, had helped secure this influence.

Colonel Holmes's memo left no doubt as to his perception of the motives of the young Bill Clinton:

> There have been many unanswered questions as to the circumstances surrounding Bill Clinton's involvement with the ROTC department at the University of Arkansas. Prior to this time I have not felt the necessity for discussing the details. . . . However, present polls show that there is the imminent danger to our country of a draft dodger becoming Commander-in-Chief of the Armed Forces of the United States. . . .
>
> This account would not have been necessary had Bill Clinton been completely honest with the American public concerning this matter. . . .
>
> Bill Clinton came to see me at my home in 1969 to discuss his desire to enroll in the ROTC program. . . . We engaged in an extensive, approximately two hour interview. At no time during this long conversation . . . did he inform me of his involvement, participation, and actually organizing protests against the United States involvement in South East Asia. . . .
>
> The next day I began to receive phone calls regarding Bill Clinton's draft status. I was informed by the draft board that it was of interest to Senator Fulbright's office that Bill Clinton, a Rhodes Scholar, should be admitted to the ROTC program. I received several such calls.

> The general message conveyed by the draft board to me was that Senator Fulbright's office was putting pressure on them and that they needed my help. I then made the necessary arrangements to enroll Mr. Clinton. . . .
>
> I was not "saving" him from serving his country, as he erroneously thanked me for in his letter from England (dated December 3, 1969). I was making it possible for a Rhodes Scholar to serve in the military as an officer.
>
> In retrospect I see that Mr. Clinton had no intention of following through with his agreement to join the Army ROTC program at the University of Arkansas or to attend the University of Arkansas Law School. I had explained to him the necessity of enrolling at the University of Arkansas as a student in order to be eligible to take the ROTC program at the University. He never enrolled at the University of Arkansas, but instead enrolled at Yale after attending Oxford. I believe that he purposely deceived me, using the possibility of joining the ROTC as a ploy to work with the draft board to delay his induction and get a new draft classification. . . .
>
> These actions cause me to question both his patriotism and his integrity.

Clinton called the allegations "absolutely untrue." But, on 4 September, he reversed himself, claiming that he had only learned of his uncle's influence six months before from Lt. Comdr. Trice Ellis, Jr. Clinton claimed that he was not contradicting his statement of just a few days before. What he meant, he said, was that he had not known about the influence when it had occurred. The reversal was published by the *Arkansas Democrat-Gazette* on 4 September.

All of this finally motivated the national news media to run the story. ABC and CBS reported it on the evening newscasts, but NBC delayed the story until 6 September. The *Washington Post* and the *New York Times* reported it, but on inside pages. On 15 September, NBC and ABC revisited the topic. Amazingly, in all of these stories, the influence of Senator Fulbright was played down or not mentioned. The facts about Fulbright's influence had been available since March, yet on "This Week with David Brinkley" on 20 September, Cokie Roberts, George Will, and Sam Donaldson—three of the most well-informed people in America—seemed to think it was a new revelation. The media had done its job well.

On 26 September, the *Los Angeles Times* reported that Cliff Jackson had arranged a meeting between Clinton and his mother and the head of the draft board to ask that his draft notice be rescinded. Such a meeting refuted all of Clinton's earlier assertions that he knew nothing about efforts on his behalf. The story also quoted a letter written from Fulbright's aide thanking Colonel Holmes "for agreeing to make room for Clinton in his already filled unit." This clinched the idea that political pull had been used to gain special privileges for Clinton. The *New York Times* gave this story four paragraphs and did not mention the thank-you letter. The *Washington Post* ran a longer story, but when it quoted the letter, it omitted the words "already filled."

Time's Advocacy

It is *Time* magazine's coverage that takes the cake. Correspondent Strobe Talbott, a friend of Clinton's back when all this had been going on, argued that Clinton had done nothing wrong and that he wasn't technically a draft dodger. This despite the fact that Talbott admits in the same article that he himself received a medical deferment that wasn't on the up-and-up. Talbott reported that Clinton dropped the option of entering the ROTC out of moral concerns but failed to mention that this attack of conscience came after Clinton knew he wouldn't be drafted. Cliff Jackson attempted to set things straight in a letter to the magazine, in which he called Talbott "one of the chief architects" of Clinton's scheme to avoid the draft. Jackson said he specifically remembered Talbott and Clinton discussing a plan to keep Clinton out of the war.

Quayle, by Contrast

Had the media devoted too much attention to the allegations of Clinton's draft-dodging?

When Dan Quayle had been nominated by George Bush in 1988, the networks alone broadcast ninety-three stories on the senator in a twelve-day period. This is in addition to the attention paid Quayle during the Republican National Convention during that period. As the Center for Media and Public Affairs points out, coverage of Quayle took up more than one-fourth of all network news time during this period. And, what did all these stories focus on?

Fifty of the ninety-three stories focused on Quayle's National Guard duty, with thirty of these focusing on the question of whether he had used his family's influence to avoid the draft. Nineteen stories dealt with Quayle's privileged family background. Nineteen more focused on the political strategy involved in Quayle's selection, most focusing on Bush's attempts to overcome the gender gap. Eighteen of these stories attempted to evaluate Quayle's impact on Bush's election chances. Thirteen stories covered Quayle's relationship with ex-lobbyist and *Playboy* pin-up Paula Parkinson, and ten stories mentioned Quayle's good looks. Out of ninety-three stories, only fifteen discussed

Quayle's career in Congress and talked about his position on the issues. This was the same electronic media who, four years later, would call character issues "negative" and insist that we focus only on the issues.

The details of Quayle's case were totally different. Quayle had not received his draft notice at the time he enlisted in the Indiana Guard, meaning that he did not break any law as Clinton had done. Neither did he receive a deferment of any kind, much less one under false pretenses as Clinton had done. Unlike Clinton, he did actually serve in the guard. Despite the great amount of media scrutiny, no evidence was ever produced to support the claim that Quayle had used any influence to secure his place in the guard. Besides, Quayle was running only for vice-president.

Nevertheless, the *New York Times* of 19 September, which finally ran the story on Clinton concerning evidence that had been available for months, ran an accompanying story about Dan Quayle and the National Guard that suggested that the two cases were equivalent.

Lingering Questions

There are other details of Clinton's effort to avoid the draft which failed to capture national attention. Before receiving his ROTC deferment, Clinton had tried to join both the air force and the navy officer training programs, only to be turned down because of poor eyesight and hearing. This means, of course, that he was probably physically ineligible to enter the ROTC.

When Clinton returned from Oxford in the summer of 1969, he went to the draft board office to confront Opal Ellis, the executive secretary, who was apparently not as cooperative as the board itself. "He told me he was too well educated to go [to Vietnam]," Ms. Ellis told the *Wall Street Journal*. Clinton told her "he was going to fix my wagon . . . pull every string he could think of." Imagine the uproar if someone had accused Quayle of such elitist, threatening language.

Ms. Ellis says the draft board was lenient with Clinton because "we were proud to have a Hot Springs boy with a Rhodes Scholarship." What is not well-known is the fact that Bill Clinton was one of the few in his class who failed to complete his degree at Oxford that the scholarship was paying for. Instead, in 1970, the year after he was no longer in danger of being drafted, he left Oxford and enrolled in Yale Law School. Had Clinton accepted the scholarship in the first place because it seemed to offer protection against the draft?

With all of this, we have not even touched on Clinton's failure to tell the truth about his antiwar activities. "I have said repeatedly that I was in two or three marches during the course of my life as an opponent of the Vietnam war," he said. "I did go to a couple of rallies. . . . I was not a big organizer of antiwar activities." But, in the famous 1969 letter to Colonel Holmes, Clinton states, "I went to Washington to work in the national headquarters of the Moratorium, then to England to organize the Americans here for demonstrations Oct. 25 and Nov. 16." Father Richard McSorley, a pacifist priest who knew Clinton at Georgetown, told, in a 1977 book entitled *Peace Eyes*, about attending an antiwar demonstration in London: "As I was waiting for the ceremony to begin, Bill Clinton of Georgetown, then studying as a Rhodes Scholar at Oxford, came up and welcomed me. He was one of the organizers."

Conclusion

Objectively speaking, George Bush may have underestimated the sympathy of baby boomers to those who opposed the Vietnam War. And, those who have examined the evidence cannot doubt that Clinton's opposition to the war was sincere and well thought-out and not merely knee-jerk anti-Americanism and anti-authoritarianism. The real question was not what Clinton did twenty years earlier, but whether or not he had lied about it to the people of Arkansas and then the people of America.

The evidence clearly shows he did, yet the media hid the evidence of that so well that an election day exit poll showed that 67 percent of the public thought Bush had lied about Iran-Contra, while only 52 percent thought Clinton had lied about his efforts to dodge the draft. Assuming for the sake of argument that both had been dishonest, why the difference? The answer can only be that the media had focused on the evidence against Bush more than it had on the evidence against Clinton.

Did the media really do so? And if so, did it do so on purpose? Consider this comment by *Newsweek*'s Eleanor Clift on "The McLaughlin Group" on 12 September after all the evidence had been made public: "There is no evidence that Bill Clinton has lied. He's done nothing illegal. He has what I would call the politician's disease. He has tailored the truth to adapt to the reality of running in a conservative southern state." So "tailoring the truth" is not the same thing as lying? No wonder our news reporting is distorted.

Chapter Five

Dan Quayle v. Murphy Brown

On 19 May, Vice-President Dan Quayle made a speech to the Commonwealth Club in San Francisco. Just weeks after the riots in Los Angeles that had resulted from the Rodney King police brutality trial, he talked about the problems facing urban America—violence, crime, and the dissolution of the family. His speech lasted forty-five paragraphs, and toward the end was this comment, spoken in a deliberate, unemotional tone:

> It doesn't help matters when prime time TV has Murphy Brown, a character who supposedly epitomizes today's intelligent, highly paid professional woman, mocking the importance of fathers by bearing a child alone and calling it just another lifestyle choice. I know it's not fashionable to talk about moral values, but we need to do it.

The media reaction was incredible. CNN and "CNN Headline News" led with the story all day the next day, and all three networks covered it that night. Local newscasts and newspapers around the country covered the "controversy," and the nighttime comedians waded in as expected. The flurry of media attention surpassed even that given the Gennifer Flowers story several months before. The possibility that a leading presidential candidate had engaged in a twelve-year-long extramarital affair got less attention than a serious statement by the vice-president of the United States concerning what he perceived to be a moral decline of America.

Most reasonable people were amazed at the media attention paid to a story that seemed both unimportant and ludicrous. Canadian prime minister Mulroney had been meeting with President Bush, and Bush had to apologize to him for the number of questions during their press conference concerning Quayle's comment. Even if Quayle's comment deserved legitimate attention, the distortion of the story by the media represented a coordinated effort to ridicule and discredit the Republican ticket in an election year.

This distortion took several forms. First, the so-called controversy was entirely media created and, thus, not a true controversy. Second, the media gave the impression that Quayle's "attack" on Murphy Brown had been far stronger than it had actually been. Third, in an effort to make the comment appear ill-advised, the media falsely claimed that the White House had attempted to "distance" itself from the statement. Fourth, Quayle's comment was quickly misinterpreted to suggest that a) he had attacked single mothers, b) he had contradicted his prolife stance, c) he had blamed the L.A. riots on "Murphy Brown," and d) he had attacked Murphy Brown as if she were a real person. Fifth, in virtually all its reporting on the subject, the media implicitly took the position that Quayle's comment deserved ridicule, and they implicitly sided with those who disagreed with Quayle's comment.

CNN Story #1

All of these distortions can be seen in CNN's coverage the day after Quayle's speech. As in the case of the Gennifer Flowers story, CNN's decision to run the story all day made the story a legitimate one for the networks to cover that night.

But, there was a major difference between this story and the Gennifer Flowers story. In this case, there had been no news conference to report on. No one who had been present at Quayle's speech had called the media or the White House to complain about it. One must also ask how, on the very night of Quayle's speech, CNN already had dissenting comments from politicians such as Mario Cuomo and "Murphy Brown" creator Diane English. The answer can only be that CNN reporters went to such people, told them what Quayle had said, and asked their response. In other words, this "controversy" was started and fueled by CNN itself. The network had actively participated in the creation of the story it was reporting on, a violation of professional ethics.

To see this, let's look at CNN's coverage the day after the speech, beginning with a short headline story from that morning:

> **CNN Anchor:** Vice-President Dan Quayle caused a controversy because of remarks he made about the popular television series "Murphy Brown." In a speech in San Francisco yesterday, Quayle lashed out at the T.V. character played by Candice Bergen for having a baby out of wedlock. He says the story line denigrates the importance of fatherhood and the American family. People at the White House, including Quayle's boss, are trying to downplay the remarks.

Bush: One of the things that concerns me deeply is the fact that there're an awful lot of broken families, and so that's really the kind of guidance I would place on that. I'm not going to get into the details of a very popular television show.

(*The anchor then reads a quotation that appears on the screen by "Diane English, Co-creator, Murphy Brown"*): If the vice-president thinks it's disgraceful for an unmarried woman to bear children, and if he believes that a woman cannot adequately raise a child without a father, then he'd better make sure abortion remains safe and legal.

Notice that two-thirds of the story is negative toward Quayle: first, by suggesting that the White House has left him on his own in this matter; second, by allowing a response by the television show's creator. But, Bush's remarks, far from trying to "play down" Quayle's comment, show that he shares Quayle's concern for the state of the American family. Bush's remarks merely indicate that he doesn't wish to get caught up in a controversy over a fictional character. Also, notice how well-crafted Diane English's response is—this is hardly an off-the-cuff response. Ms. English was clearly told about Quayle's remarks and then given time to draft a response.

CNN Story #2

Now let's look at CNN's story an hour later:

Anchor: Vice-President Dan Quayle blasted the popular television series "Murphy Brown" in a speech last night, saying declining moral values are glorified on T.V. and unwed fathers need to take responsibility. He blamed the Los Angeles riots on the ethic that excuses lifestyle choices like those on "Murphy Brown." The president today used softer language.

(*Same sound bite from Bush.*)

Anchor: Bush spokesman Marlin Fitzwater says he enjoys "Murphy Brown," and it's helpful, he said, that she's demonstrating prolife values. An hour earlier, though, Fitzwater seconded Quayle's comment, saying, quoting here, "Glorification of life as an unwed mother does not do good service to those who aren't highly paid anchorwomen."

Fitzwater's words were not contradictory, as this story suggests. His original statement certainly was not an effort to "distance" the White House from Quayle. His second statement was in response to a reporter's question asking if Quayle would rather Murphy Brown had an abortion. What Quayle wanted, of course, was for Murphy not to get pregnant out of wedlock. This was the first of the misinterpretations of Quayle's comment.

CNN Story #3

Now let's look at a story by Gloria Hilliard later that day:

Hilliard: On Monday, when single mom Murphy Brown delivered her baby on prime time, Vice-President Dan Quayle delivered this salvo:

(*Quayle's comment from his speech.*)

Hilliard: CBS had no comment, but "Murphy Brown" producer Diane English said this:

(*Same quotation on screen.*)

Hilliard: If Candice Bergen's character had chosen to have an abortion, that certainly would have caused some controversy, controversy not unfamiliar to Hollywood. In 1972, when Maude chose to have an abortion, it caused an uproar. A decade later, CBS was the target of protests once again when, in an episode of "Cagney & Lacey" dealing with the bombing of an abortion clinic, Mary Beth Lacey disclosed she'd had an abortion as a teenager.

Hollywood producer Stephen Bochco, who produced the controversial docudrama "Roe v. Wade," called the vice-president's statement "cavalier."

Bochco: I think they portray a real simplistic view of our world and the society in which we live.

Hilliard: That is the feeling of *Time* magazine's media correspondent, who believes T.V. is a mirror of society and in that reflection women are increasingly being seen as strong and independent. Susan Carpentar-McMillan of the Pro-Family Media Coalition says she agrees with the vice-president's comments.

Carpentar-McMillan: . . . that we need a mother and a father to raise the next generation. The so-called–I call them antiwomen feminists, antifamily feminists–have done a great job of mucking up this country over the last twenty years.

Hilliard (*on screen*)**:** In an ideal world perhaps, but even in a fictional T.V. storyline, working single mother Murphy Brown seems to epitomize a more realistic picture of today's working woman, albeit most don't have it as good as T.V.'s favorite anchorwoman.

Read Hilliard's closing statement again. In this story, three people have disagreed with Quayle's statement. One person then agrees with it, *only to be contradicted by the reporter herself.* The final score, then, is four against one. Notably, Carpentar-McMillan is the only expert source outside the White House that CNN found throughout the day who agreed with Quayle's statement.

CNN Story #4

Brian Jenkins: In the affluent suburb of Ridgewood, New Jersey, few people seem ready to buy Dan Quayle's argument that poverty in the big cities can be blamed on a breakdown of morals.

White man: I think he should concentrate more on what's going on in America rather than what's on prime time television.

Jenkins: The vice-president's pot shot at T.V.'s Murphy Brown to many here seemed off the mark.

White woman: You're talking about a high-powered T.V. anchor who makes a very good living and who's not on welfare and who doesn't have to worry about how she's going to make ends meet. . . .

Jenkins: Still, Mr. Quayle's larger message may have hit home with most of Ridgewood's residents.

Older white woman: We're trying to get back to family life. Normal family life; let's put it that way.

Young black man: Once the family starts breaking down, you get problems like that, where the kids don't grow up and learn the right values.

Jenkins: But observers of the American scene wonder what sort of family is "right" or "normal" today.

Judsen Cullbreth, Editor, *Working Woman*: It's not one stereotype any more. You can't look at one picture. There're no icons like Ozzie and Harriet anymore. Murphy Brown is as legitimate as Barbara Bush.

Alan Wolfe, New School for Social Research: Twice as many families in the United States conform to the Murphy Brown model as compared to what we'd call the Ozzie and Harriet model.

Jenkins: Most of the mothers who come to pick up preschoolers at Ridgewood Presbyterian Church do have husbands at home, but none of these women are prepared to pass moral judgements on single mothers in the inner cities.

Mother: Why are no fathers at home in these families? It's because of lack of employment and opportunity. . . .

Jenkins: So the question, says the church's pastor, is how to give all types of families a fighting chance.

Rev. Leland Gartrell: What is it that will help society stick together, and grow, and develop in order to enable every person as well as household and community to have a great life in the world that we share?

Jenkins: A world that keeps changing, even in suburbia.

Looking back over this report, you'll find that Jenkins cannot decide whether Ridgewood residents agree with Quayle or not. He states that "few people buy" Quayle's comments, but then says they do agree with his "larger message." Notice, however, that the second person quoted, a woman who supposedly doesn't buy the message, doesn't actually disagree. Jenkins, then, was able to find only one person who specifically disagreed with Quayle's statement.

Jenkins then turns to "observers of the American scene," but he fails to quote anyone taking a conservative view. The two quotations we do hear have several problems. Both Cullbreth and Wolfe point out that there are many broken homes in America today, which is precisely what Quayle is warning us about. These two are guilty of circular reasoning; they are saying that the existence of so many fragmented households is the very reason we can't try to avoid fragmented households. Cullbreth's claim that a woman having a child out of wedlock is as legitimate as a traditional family is certainly an open question, and there are no doubt as many who would disagree with her as with Quayle.

Jenkins's comment about passing "moral judgement" on single mothers in the inner cities is the beginning of another misinterpretation of Quayle's comment. Quayle had not passed moral judgement on single mothers of any type. He had complained about the decline of the traditional family unit and had simply suggested that Hollywood should not glamorize single motherhood.

CNN showed Democratic senator Patrick Leahy of Vermont saying, in a discussion on the Los Angeles riots, "It's an Alice in Wonderland situation. How they can say this takes responsibility from the administration's actions, by blaming a fictional character . . . is more than I can understand." This suggested that Quayle had blamed the riots on Murphy Brown, another misinterpretation widely repeated in the media.

The language of the CNN anchors and reporters was more virulent than was Quayle's. Quayle "blasted" and "lashed out" at the television show, they said. He "delivered a salvo." One intro even said, "Dan Quayle draws fire for trying to hang a scarlet letter on a TV character." David French's commentary on 21 May called Quayle's comment "attack politics White House-style." Attacking whom? Isn't French being a bit over-protective of a fictional character?

But, the real kicker comes when anchor David Goodnow sums up the story: "Democratic presidential frontrunner Bill Clinton said he doesn't approve of television showing illegitimate births, but he said that's far less a problem than depictions of violence." In other words, Clinton agreed with Quayle's comment.

The Hypocrisy, the Hypocrisy

Clinton was not the only one. On 8 June, *U.S. News and World Report* published several statements made before Quayle's comment that did not receive the same response:

"Every night, prime-time television assails [children] with mindless sitcoms and soap operas that present materialism and unrelenting self-gratification as the only goals worth pursuing." That was from New York governor Mario Cuomo, a man who said that Quayle's comment represented a "comic book mentality."

"The basic moral standards of the society are dropping. Somebody must say that babies making babies is morally wrong." That's from Jesse Jackson, the man who claimed that Quayle's comment had been an attack on single mothers.

"Governments can't raise children, people do, and the people who bring children into this world should all bear responsibility for raising them." That one, again, was from Bill Clinton.

There were also other conservatives who had said much the same thing without causing a fire storm of controversy. In January, Louis Sullivan, the secretary of Health and Human Services, delivered a speech to the Council on Families in America. Sullivan, who is black, said that the "male absence from family life" was the greatest problem facing America today. He pointed out that children brought up in single-parent families are five times more likely to be poor and twice as likely to drop out of school as are those in two-parent families.

But, the most notable statement made before Quayle's was an article in the *Washington Post* on 10 May by Barbara Defoe Whitehead entitled "What is Murphy Brown Saying?" "For the first time," said Whitehead, a researcher for the liberal Institute for American Values, "a prime-time television show will celebrate unwed motherhood as a glamorous lifestyle option." The absence of a father hurts children, she said. "The plain truth is that every child needs both a mother and a father. A father cannot be replaced by a paycheck, or by a therapist, or even a Murphy Brown."

Notice the similarity between Whitehead's "lifestyle option" and Quayle's "lifestyle choice." Whitehead later learned that the Quayle staff had used her article as a source for Quayle's speech. In other words, Quayle was only repeating what had already been published in the liberal *Post*. Yet, the *Post* joined the rest of the media in attacking him.

Unlike Quayle's speech, Whitehead's article really did attack Murphy Brown directly. Yet, there were no CNN headlines, no calls to the *Post* editor asking if the paper wished to "distance" itself from her remarks, and no claims that Whitehead was attacking single mothers.

If all these people had been saying basically the same thing, one must ask why Quayle's comments caused the uproar they did. The answer can only be that the media saw this as a way to make Quayle look silly. Quayle had long ago joined other Republican vice-presidents–Nixon, Agnew, Ford–in being caricatured by the media in order to damage his political viability.

The most hypocritical response to Quayle's comment came from none other than Hillary Clinton. "We don't need Dan Quayle telling us what the family ought to be," she said on at least two occasions. But, Hillary, in her legal writings and activist efforts, had long been seeking to alter the legal definition and standing of the American family. Apparently, we don't need our nationally elected leaders telling us what the family ought to be, but we do need a lawyer from Little Rock telling us what the family ought to be.

What Quayle Actually Said

What was in this speech that gained so much notoriety? Why would the vice-president of the United States give a speech focusing on a single television show, no matter how disgusting it might be? Shouldn't the vice-president be focusing on real issues that have a real effect on Americans?

Indeed, he should, and indeed, he did. Contrary to the impression given by the media and by Quayle's political opponents, calling his speech of 19 May a "Murphy Brown speech" is a complete misnomer. The speech was not about "Murphy Brown," nor was it about the influence of Hollywood and other popular culture. It was a speech about the statistically proven erosion of the traditional family unit and its effect on young Americans, particularly those trapped in the poverty of the inner cities.

The speech begins with a decidedly inclusionary tone. Quayle had recently been on a mission to Japan, and, while there, he had been asked repeatedly about the recent Los Angeles riots. The Japanese, who consider their cultural homogeneity to be a strength, asked if the riots were not an inevitable result of America's ethnic diversity. Quayle assured them that such was not the case and that America's ethnic diversity was its strength. But, Quayle points out, we do need to answer the many questions raised by the riots.

Quayle begins by blasting those who have excused the riots or said "I told you so," all as a ploy to secure increased government funding. "To apologize or in any way to excuse what happened is wrong. It is a betrayal of all those people equally outraged and equally disadvantaged who did not loot and did not riot–and who were in many cases victims of the rioters." He then turns to what he sees as the real problem:

> In a nutshell: I believe the lawless social anarchy which we saw is directly related to the breakdown of family structure, personal responsibility and social order in too many areas of our society. For the poor the situation is compounded by a welfare ethos that impedes individual efforts to move ahead in society, and hampers their ability to take advantage of the opportunities America offers. If we don't succeed in addressing these fundamental problems, and in restoring basic values, any attempt to fix what's broken will fail.

Quayle says he is confident we won't fail because of how much progress has been made in the last twenty-five years. He talks about the advances made by black Americans, citing statistics. But, he also acknowledges the development of a seemingly permanent underclass.

> . . . in this dynamic, prosperous nation, poverty has traditionally been a stage through which people pass on their way to joining the great middle class. And if one generation didn't get

> very far up the ladder—their ambitious, better-educated children would.
>
> But the underclass seems to be a new phenomenon. It is a group whose members are dependent on welfare for very long stretches, and whose men are often drawn into lives of crime. There is far too little upward mobility, because the underclass is disconnected from the rules of society. And these problems have, unfortunately, been particularly acute for black Americans.

Quayle cites statistics to show the decline of the family in the black community. He talks about the tendency of the baby boomer generation to discard traditional values, seek self-gratification, and escape responsibility. He suggests that those in the middle class had the resources to indulge such ideas, then return to traditional values and decent jobs. Those in the underclass, with less to fall back on, found it more difficult to escape the results of such indulgences.

> The intergenerational poverty that troubles us so much today is predominantly a poverty of values. Our inner cities are filled with children having children; with people who have not been able to take advantage of educational opportunities; with people who are dependent on drugs or the narcotic of welfare.
>
> Unless we change the basic rules of society in our inner cities, we cannot expect anything else to change. . . . For the government, transforming underclass culture means that our policies and programs must create a different incentive system. Our policies must be premised on, and must reinforce, values such as: family, hard work, integrity and personal responsibility.

Quayle then goes on to talk about government's responsibility to maintain order. He points out that 84 percent of crimes committed by blacks are committed against blacks. Quayle talks about the "empowerment programs" that the Bush administration has prepared for the inner cities. These proposals are hardly controversial–welfare reform, raising educational standards, creating enterprise zones, and providing job training.

Then, and only then, does Quayle turn in earnest to the subject of the declining family:

> Children need love and discipline. They need mothers and fathers. A welfare check is not a husband. The state is not a father. It is from parents that children learn how to behave in society; it is from parents above all that children come to understand values and themselves as men and women, mothers and fathers.
>
> And for those concerned about children growing up in poverty, we should know this: marriage is probably the best anti-poverty program of all. Among families headed by married couples today, there is a poverty rate of 5.7%. But 33.4% of families headed by a single mother are in poverty today.

Earlier, when discussing law and order, Quayle had spoken of the dilemma of the single mother raising her children in the ghetto, not being sure they would live through the day. Surely in this speech, Quayle has shown compassion, not disdain, for the problems of the single mother living in poverty.

He goes on to talk about gangs, about teenage pregnancy, and, yes, about the influence of popular culture on the loss of traditional values. His total references to popular culture include the Murphy Brown comment and one other sentence about the "cultural leaders in Hollywood, network T.V., [and] the national newspapers." He closes by calling repeatedly for a "national debate" on traditional moral values. And, he pledges to help George Bush lead such a debate.

This speech is no great feat of oratory–phrases such as "We are a nation of laws, not looting" are unlikely to take a permanent place beside the best of Abraham Lincoln and Winston Churchill. Nor is the speech controversial or surprising in its analysis of society's ills–the need for a return to traditional values had been a standard Republican theme since the 1960s. Nevertheless, Quayle's remarks were both timely and weighty. Given all of this, what motivated the media to pull out a single, nonessential sentence and use it to distort and discredit Quayle's message?

Bashing Family Values

As we've already seen, the first reaction of the media was to bash the idea of family values. This continued long after the initial brouhaha, with a solid media consensus that the issue was either unimportant or mere politics on the part of the Republicans.

Take, for example, the 19 August "CBS Evening News" "Eye On America" segment. This story, which lasted two minutes and fifty-six seconds, talked to people in Clarksdale, Miss. The gist of the story, of course, was that family values was merely a political ploy by the Republicans. Amazingly, in this small Mississippi town, CBS couldn't find a single individual who agreed with the Republican message.

John Chancellor, on the opening night of the Democratic National Convention, said this: "Family values in our constitutional system should be the responsibility of the clergy, not the presidency. But for a number of years now, the Republicans have been beating up on the Democrats with the issue of family values." Chancellor is wrong, of course–family values are a societal, not merely a religious, issue.

Besides, since when did the media gain the authority to declare which issues are legitimate and on which issues candidates may campaign? If people do not respond to the issue of family values, why not let the Republicans campaign on it and lose as a result? Why would you need to discredit the issue unless you knew that people really were responding to it?

Embracing Family Values

Unfortunately for the Democrats, and in marked contrast to the disdain shown the subject by the media, the polls showed that the Republican talk about family values was quite popular with middle America. "They [the Democrats] are a little worried about it," Andrea Mitchell stated during the Republican National Convention on 19 August, "because they think it is a powerful issue that will bring home the Reagan Democrats and also firm up George Bush's base."

Thus, while the first reaction of the media and the Democrats had been to bash family values, their second reaction was to embrace them. At the Democratic National Convention, Bill Clinton spent the first fifteen minutes of his acceptance speech talking about family values.

When her husband had been a presidential contender in the 1988 primaries, Tipper Gore had made headlines by protesting the violence and obscenity of rock lyrics. Along with Susan Baker, wife of Secretary of State James Baker, she had formed the Parents' Music Resource Center to fight for mandatory record labeling. When family values became the issue of the 1992 election, Tipper's campaign was resurrected as a shining example of the Democrats' commitment to moral values. An August story in the *New York Times*, for example, championed her work.

But, as the *Times* also pointed out, although the issue "played well in Tennessee," it did not endear Ms.

Gore to the entertainment industry or the more liberal members of the Democratic party, both important sources of campaign contributions. The result was that Tipper began to backpedal on the issue even as her efforts were being lauded. Her group retreated from mandatory labeling, accepting voluntary labeling instead. The group issued no statement about the controversial song "Cop Killer." Instead, as the *Times* reported, she "has begun to win over the music industry."

"Cop Killer," by the way, was a Time Warner release, as was Madonna's *Sex* book, the rap song "KKK Bitch" (the title referring to Tipper herself), and the rap song thought to have contributed to the murder of a Texas state trooper. Why did Tipper and her husband not take on Time Warner if they were so committed to family values? Well, Time Warner was a major underwriter of the Democratic National Convention to the tune of more than four hundred thousand dollars. Time Warner co-chairman Steven Ross gave more than one hundred thousand dollars to Democrats between 1988 and 1992. Columnist Morton Kondrake found that Ted Field, the head of a Time Warner subsidiary, had also donated one hundred thousand dollars to the Democratic party, as well as being a supporter of the liberal group People for the American Way. In other words, money made from the violent rap songs and books such as Madonna's *Sex* were going to help elect Clinton and Gore.

At the same time, Democrats publicly embraced family values. But, they did so by redefining them. They pointed to such sweeping legislation as the family leave bill and the day care bill as examples of their commitment to family values. Of course, sweeping new government regulations and government care of children was precisely *not* what Dan Quayle had in mind.

Who Needs Families?

One of the surest signs that the Republicans were winning with the family values issues was a sudden, sporadic effort by the media to discredit the very idea of the family. "Experts Rethinking Views on the Traditional Family," read the headline in the 21 September *Washington Post*, "Effects of Broken Homes May be Overstated." This article—written by Malcolm Gladwell—was widely reprinted in newspapers around the country. It reported that the importance of an unbroken home to proper childhood development "is undergoing a searching re-evaluation by social scientists."

One doesn't have to be a social scientist to see the flaws in the article. The first clue is in the disclaimers which make it clear that there is no scientific consensus that the traditional family is not important. "The new evidence is by no means conclusive," we are told. "Researchers stress that the recent findings do not mean that absent fathers and divorce pose no problems to children." What the article does say is that those problems may be less than were previously thought by social scientists based on studies conducted in the fifties and sixties, a fact that may bring little comfort to a three-year-old child who watches her father walk out the door. But, while the evidence is "by no means conclusive," the three experts quoted in the article had clearly already drawn their own conclusions. Amazingly, the investigative powers of the *Post* were unable to locate a single expert to offer a balancing view.

The article is full of flawed logic. "By comparing children of divorce in poor families with those from well-off families, researchers found that problems previously thought to be caused by the absence of the father's emotional and psychological contribution to the family may be related to the loss of income." Doesn't that still mean the problems are the result of a broken home? Isn't the high poverty level of single-parent families a common liberal lament? "They also have seen that children of divorce start having high levels of emotional problems before their parents' divorce. That suggests that the children's problems are less the result of the absence of a father than the conflict between parents in a traditional setting." But, households that have such severe problems that they end in divorce are not what we mean by a "traditional setting." Using households that are breaking apart as a sample group to judge households which do not is hardly scientific.

Other Gaffes

The media, needless to say, was not through with Quayle. A few months after the Murphy Brown speech, Quayle appeared on "Larry King Live." King asked him what he would do if his daughter grew up and got pregnant and decided to have an abortion. This was, of course, one of those "Have you stopped beating your wife?" questions, the kind that make you sound guilty whether you answer yes or no. If Quayle says that he would stand by his daughter, he sounds prochoice. If he says he would not, he sounds like a poor father, and after all his talk of family values.

Quayle replied that he would counsel his daughter against having an abortion, but that he would stand by her if she decided to have one. Legally speaking, there was nothing else he could do—the hypothetical question concerned a grown daughter undergoing a legal procedure.

The next day, there was another flurry of media attention. New York governor Mario Cuomo said that Quayle had "come out pro-choice" with his statement. Marilyn Quayle quickly jumped in to assure everyone that, should her daughter become pregnant, she would carry the child to term.

All of this was absurd. No one who watched the interview came away with the impression that Quayle had wavered in his position. The most he could have been accused of would be holding a double standard, but even this would be a distortion. Standing by your daughter when she has an abortion against your will does not make you a proponent of abortion any more than standing by your son at his rape trial makes you a proponent of rape.

This occurred after the most famous Quayle gaffe of all. While visiting a school, Quayle was reading words from flashcards, which the students would then spell on the board. When a boy wrote *potato* on the board, Quayle told him to go back and add an *e* to the end of the word. The media exploded with hilarity. The vice-president didn't know how to spell *potato*. The joke was repeated in news commentary, in opposition speeches, in comedy routines, and on "Murphy Brown" literally for years.

What the media failed to mention was that the flashcard Quayle had been holding had the word misspelled. Glancing down at the misspelled word in the glare of television lights, anyone might overlook such a mistake.

Perhaps the most deliberate and mean-spirited misinterpretation of Quayle's words came just before his debate with Al Gore in October. Quayle joked that, even though his opponent had attended the finest private schools in Washington while he had gone to public schools in Indiana, he would still try to do his best. This is clearly a joke–a humorous way of pointing out that his opponent was actually more privileged than he, despite the images created by the media. The media that laughed so hard at the Murphy Brown comment and the potato joke suddenly lost their sense of humor. Reporters and commentators quite seriously accused him of cutting down the public school system.

After the election, Al Gore, Jr. was touring a historical site. With the television cameras rolling, he pointed at some busts and asked, "Now, who are these people?" His guide, looking at the bust Gore was pointing to, said, "Well, that's George Washington." Again, the media had exhausted its sense of humor, and the gaffe went unreported except for the "Rush Limbaugh Show."

Yes, Dan Quayle was our national punchline for four years. Did he deserve the treatment he received? One can answer this by asking, what was it that Dan Quayle actually did wrong as vice-president? What task did he fail to perform; what diplomatic faux pas did he commit; what scandal was he involved in? The answer, of course, is that he did nothing wrong. His only sin was that his political positions differed greatly from those of the average journalist, earning him their scorn and thus their ridicule. The journalists who turned Dan Quayle into a national joke and a political liability because he couldn't spell *potato* were the very ones who complained that the Republican campaign was negative and didn't focus on the issues. The same journalists who were complaining that Hillary Clinton's words were being quoted selectively and distorted were busy doing the same thing to the words of Dan Quayle.

One final note: Murphy Brown's baby played a major role in the storyline of the television show in the year following the uproar. But in the 1993-94 season, the producers decided to relegate the child to an occasional reference or brief appearance. They had discovered that Dan Quayle was right: single motherhood is neither glamorous nor funny.

Chapter Six

The Hillary Factor

During the primaries, Bill Clinton said, "If I get elected president, it will be an unprecedented partnership, far more than Franklin Roosevelt and Eleanor." At another point, Clinton said "We often joke that the campaign slogan should be 'Buy One, Get One Free.'" Hillary said, "If you elect him, you get me. It's a two-for-one blue plate special." When asked if she would be interested in the vice-presidency, Hillary said, "I'm not interested in attending a lot of funerals around the world. I want maneuverability . . . I want to get deeply involved in solving problems." In other words, the position of vice-president would not be enough for her.

Such comments, and Hillary's clear record of success in activist causes and in her own career, caused euphoria among feminists and the media. Here was a "new kind of political wife" we were told, a "role model for the next generation of women." Here was a first lady who would not be mere window dressing, but a partner in setting public policy. The contrast to the grandmotherly Barbara Bush could not have been more pronounced.

But, if Hillary were to be a "co-president," or to play a significant part in the setting of public policy, then her qualifications and her views should be subject to the same public scrutiny as her husband's. To excuse her from such scrutiny would be sexist–it would be letting her off easy or suggesting that her views are not important because she is a woman. Feminists, one would think, would not only welcome such scrutiny, they would demand it.

What happened instead contradicted everything feminism stands for, yet feminists stood by silently. First, the media failed to give the views or past record of Hillary Rodham Clinton the scrutiny they deserved. Second, those who did examine her views were denounced for attacking a "candidate's wife." Then, in a supreme display of hypocrisy, and to the dismay of many feminists, Hillary was silenced by the campaign handlers and made over into the image of the quintessential yuppie housewife.

The media that denounced Quayle's views on family values as mere politics said not a word about Hillary's new plaid skirts and headbands. The liberal columnists who championed Hillary's abilities and accomplishments paradoxically turned on anyone who looked too closely at what she had actually done over the years. Why this inconsistency? The only explanation is that the media knew full well that Hillary's views were not mainstream. They therefore embarked on a determined campaign to hide or distort those views and to discredit any who attempted to set the record straight by calling them "sexist."

Hillary's Past

And, what is the record? As you read this short summation of her activities and writings, notice how little of it you learned from the media during the campaign.

In 1987-88, Hillary served as chairman of the New World Foundation, which she herself described as being dedicated to the support of "progressive activist organizations." The foundation was ranked by the Capital Research Center as one of the country's ten most liberal. Under her leadership, the foundation gave thirty-five thousand dollars to the Christic Institute, a group that claims that the Vietnam War and the Iran-Contra affair were the work of a drug-dealing network in the CIA and the U.S. military. The Committee in Solidarity with the People of El Salvador (CISPES) received five thousand dollars. This group is the U.S. arm of the communist FMLN, which attempted to overthrow the elected government of El Salvador and killed American soldiers in the process. The foundation also gave money to the National Lawyer's Guild, which works to protect the constitutional rights of American communists.

Hillary served for six years as chairman of the Children's Defense Fund, which, incidentally, received $20 thousand in 1988 from none other than the New World Foundation. The CDF's goal is to promote liberal programs for children—children's rights, condom giveaways, and sexuality training beginning in first grade.

Perhaps most disturbing is Hillary's appointment by Jimmy Carter in 1978 to the chairmanship of the Legal Services Corporation. The purpose of the LSC is to provide legal assistance to the poor, and it is specifically prohibited from engaging in political activities. Nevertheless, under Hillary's guidance, the LSC contributed to campaigns, spent money and staff time attempting to defeat an antitax referendum in California, and even attempted to organize a nationwide network to oppose Reagan initiatives following his election. According to the *American Spectator*, the comptroller general of the General Accounting Office in 1983 issued a report chronicling the illegal activities of the LSC. Even with this report as part of the public record, not a single national news media outlet conducted an investigation into Hillary's compliance with these illegal activities.

It is important to realize that such activities comprise Hillary's credentials to take part in the setting of public policy. Normally, politicians trumpet their past activities to show they are qualified. Because first ladies don't normally take part in public policy decisions, one would expect these activities to be widely publicized in order to silence those who felt Hillary to be unqualified. But, such was not the case. Again, the reason can only be that the campaign and the media knew that Hillary's activities would be considered radical by mainstream America.

Hillary's Writings

In 1977, in the *Yale Law Journal,* Hillary's article "Children's Policies: Abandonment and Neglect" criticized Gilbert Steiner of the Brookings Institute for suggesting that government be careful about intervening in family matters:

> Steiner posits that "non-intervention serves as a basic guiding principle rather than an absolute." Steiner's rejection of absolutism is welcome, but it is his cautious attitude toward governmental involvement in child-rearing that implicitly molds his analysis. . . . There is nothing wrong with pressing for better programs for the needy, but Steiner sets his sights too low.

In a 1974 essay entitled "Children Under the Law," she proposed the abolition of the legal status of minority, the reversal of the legal presumption of the incompetence of minors, the granting of all procedural legal rights to children, and "the rejection of the legal presumption of the identity of interests between parents and their children." In the same article we learn the justification for such measures:

> The basic rationale for depriving people of rights in a dependency relationship is that certain individuals are incapable or undeserving of the right to take care of themselves and consequently need social institutions specifically designed to safe-guard their position.

From a legal standpoint, this sentence is technically correct. Most people would consider it a good thing that the family plays the role of safeguarding children. But, Hillary adds a kicker:

> Along with the family, past and present examples of such arrangements include marriage, slavery and the Indian reservation. The relative powerlessness of children makes them uniquely vulnerable to this rationale.

Again, from a legal standpoint, these are indeed examples of "dependency relationships." Defenders of Hillary therefore swear that she is not, in this passage, equating the family or marriage with slavery. But, earlier in the article she specifically compared arguments against children's rights with earlier arguments for slavery and against women's emancipation.

(Incidentally, there is one "dependency relationship" under the law which Hillary left off her list: that of mother and unborn child. She follows the standard liberal contradiction of abortion and children's rights: Parents who can kill their children before birth are allowed little control over them after birth.)

In a 1979 article entitled "Children's Rights: A Legal Perspective," she says that her opponents are silly to suggest that her ideas would "allow children to take parents to court if they were ordered to take out the garbage. Family disagreements that result in legal battles are, of course, of a more serious nature." But, as Daniel Wattenberg points out, parents are unlikely to take comfort in the idea that it is only the important decisions that will be taken out of their hands by the government. Hillary goes on to list these more important issues as "decisions about motherhood and abortion, schooling, cosmetic surgery, treatment of venereal disease, or employment." The overall thesis of her piece is that "children should have a right to be permitted to decide their own future if they are competent." And, it is judges, not parents, who will decide whether they are competent.

What's in a Name?

When Bill and Hillary Clinton were first married (and, by the way, they lived together first, another fact the media didn't mention in its many biographical sketches of the couple), Hillary kept her maiden name. The press releases following Chelsea's birth stated that "Governor Bill Clinton and Hillary Rodham" had had a child. Such blatant feminism doesn't go over well in the small towns of Arkansas, and, in the next election, Bill and Hillary were turned out of the state house. By the next election, she had ditched her goofy seventies glasses for contacts and started, for the first time in her life, wearing makeup and dressing fashionably. She had also taken her husband's name.

Or so she said. But, according to the *American Spectator*, her 1991 income tax form was filed under the name Hillary Rodham. Today, according to the Associated Press, she is listed in the White House directory under the Rs as "Hillary Rodham-Clinton." The White House correspondents cannot help but know this, yet the press refers to her as "Mrs. Clinton."

Most Americans would agree that a woman has the right to call herself whatever she chooses. But, most Americans would think little of a political wife who changes her name just to enhance her husband's political career. They would think even less of one who pretends to change her name but really doesn't. This is not a question of women's rights; it is a question of honesty. As it stands, Hillary Rodham-Clinton has lied to the public about her very name, and the media has consciously assisted her in perpetuating that lie.

Defending Hillary

There are two common misconceptions about Hillary's image problems in the 1992 campaign. The first is that the press was harsh and unfair to her. The second is that the Republicans and others launched a sexist attack on her for living the life of a modern, independent career woman.

There simply was never a time when the press attacked Hillary Clinton. In fact, the precise opposite is true. From the beginning, the media protected Hillary by hiding her more radical political positions and by blatantly defending her against her real and imaginary foes.

"From the beginning" is no exaggeration. Hillary was heard by most Americans for the first time in the famous "60 Minutes" interview following the Super Bowl in January. Steve Kroft, who conducted the interview, told Gail Sheehy that Hillary was in such control of the interview that "we found ourselves rationing her sound bites to keep her from becoming the dominant force in the interview." In other words, "60 Minutes" censored Hillary's true nature and the true balance of power between her and her husband. Even these liberal journalists were instinctively uncomfortable with Hillary's tendency to seize control.

A perfect example of the outright defense of Hillary is Albert R. Hunt's "In Fairness to the Candidate's

Wife" in the 16 July issue of the *Wall Street Journal*. This essay is filled with distortions and outright untruths. Hunt says, for example, that "the pounding against Ms. Clinton has been ferocious," but he can name as examples only articles in *Human Events* and the *American Spectator*, partisan journals that can hardly be called mainstream press. Referring to Wattenberg's article in the *Spectator*, he says this:

> It accuses her of everything from filing her 1991 tax return under her maiden name after supposedly taking her husband's following his gubernatorial defeat in 1980, to seeking to undermine the American family by pitting children against their parents. (Most of these charges concern legitimate issues; by contrast, some of the private stuff being circulated against Hillary Clinton is full of nothing but hate and venom.)

This is very confusing. Hunt suggests that Hillary does not deserve the "ferocious pounding" she is getting, but he then says that the articles he names as examples of that pounding concern mostly "legitimate issues." It is the "private stuff" that is irresponsible, he says, but he does not give us even an example of this "stuff" or tell us who is circulating it. Nor does he acknowledge that the things of which Wattenberg "accuses" Hillary are actually true. He goes on from there:

> Under scrutiny many of the more substantive charges don't hold up very well. Most are based either on writings that date back to her law school days or on grants made by groups in which she served as one of many board members.

As we have already seen, however, Hillary was more than merely "one of many board members" of the Children's Defense Fund, the Legal Services Corporation, and the New World Foundation–she was the chairman of each. This is no mere oversight on Hunt's part; later in the article he talks about her six-year chairmanship of the CDF. It is true that some of her writings "date back to her law school days," but these writings are only fifteen to twenty years old, and her later writings and speeches make it clear that her views have not changed. Certainly, she had made no effort to distance herself from those writings once they began undergoing reexamination. But, Hunt is not through yet:

> For example, she once wrote that under certain circumstances children ought to have greater legal rights to separate from their parents. But she said this should only be in extreme cases. Indeed there are situations ranging from child abuse to abandonment where this hardly seems a radical view.

Notice that it is Hunt, not Hillary, who gives the examples of child abuse and abandonment. Hunt doesn't bother to point out that Hillary's list of "extreme cases" includes such situations as the desire for cosmetic surgery, situations which would indeed seem radical to most people. In fact, Hunt, like virtually all defenders of Hillary, somehow manages to avoid quoting her at all. But, Hunt is still not through:

> Within the Clinton campaign, where not everyone is charmed by her style, knowledgeable insiders nevertheless say she is no radical.
>
> "I have never seen her push any kind of ideological agenda," says top political strategist James Carville. "My guess is she's pretty much a mainstream Democrat who feels very strongly about children's issues." That Mr. Carville, a

> plain-talking Louisiana Cajun who is appealingly anti-establishment, has such positive feelings about Hillary Clinton also undercuts the contention that she relates only to the cultural elite.

Are we to be astonished that one of the heads of the Democratic campaign can find nothing but good things to say about his candidate's spouse? Does Mr. Hunt believe us naive enough to view Carville as an objective source? Is Hunt naive enough to do so himself? If so, is he really qualified to serve as Washington bureau chief for the *Wall Street Journal*?

Hunt conveniently overlooks the fact that Carville had been part of the group who, earlier in the campaign, had threatened to walk if Hillary were not reined in. Of course, Hunt's essay was published as an editorial, and he has the right to advocate for Hillary Clinton if he so chooses. But, he does not have the right to distort the record and ignore facts in order to make his case.

The most blatant example of advocacy journalism in the entire campaign was the cover story of *Time* on 14 September. On the cover, beneath a warm, smiling picture of Hillary, is the headline "The Hillary Factor. Is She Helping or Hurting Her Husband?" One might expect from this an objective analysis of her effect on the election, backed up by statistics and comments from voters and politicians on both sides of the aisle. What one gets instead is a six-page editorial by Margaret Carlson suggesting that: a) everything the Republicans have said about Hillary is distorted or made up; b) voters dislike Hillary only because of this Republican distortion; c) the whole strategy should and will backfire on the Republicans; d) Hillary is actually a warm, loving, and religious person; and e) even if she is a barracuda, the Republican spouses are as bad or worse. Every quote from Hillary shows her at her best, every quote from Republicans shows them at their worst.

The story itself is entitled "All Eyes on Hillary." The subheading alerts the reader that the article will take a protective stance toward Hillary. "The G.O.P. hopes to gain votes by attacking her as a radical feminist who prefers the boardroom to the kitchen. But the ploy could backfire by alienating working women." Like most Hillary defenders, Carlson fails to note that Hillary really does prefer the boardroom to the kitchen and that she is, if not a radical feminist, certainly a staunch one. Nevertheless, Carlson's lead-in borrows a line directly from the Democratic campaign by saying that the Republicans are trying to turn Hillary "into 'Willary Horton' for the '92 campaign."

An idea of the integrity of the piece can be gleaned from a single paragraph:

> The foundations of the anti-Hillary campaign were carefully poured and were part of a larger effort to solidify Bush's conservative base. Republicans dug up—and seriously distorted—some of her old academic articles on children's rights. Rich Bond, the chairman of the Republican National Committee, caricatured Hillary as a lawsuit-mongering feminist who likened marriage to slavery and encouraged children to sue their parents. (She did no such thing.) Richard Nixon warned that her forceful intelligence was likely to make her husband "look like a wimp." Patrick Buchanan blasted "Clinton & Clinton" for what he claims was their agenda of abortion on demand, homosexual rights and putting women in combat.

What Buchanan "claims" was their agenda? These three items were specifically written into the Democratic platform. This was not an attack on Hillary, but on the issues, and Buchanan was in no way distorting those issues. Richard Nixon had indeed said, "If the wife comes through as being too strong and too intelligent, it makes the husband look like a wimp." But, Nixon, as he is wont to do these days, was speaking as an elder statesman, not as a partisan Republican. He was, after all, merely stating what has been a truism in American politics in the past, and he was warning Bill more than he was attacking Hillary.

Rich Bonds's words seem harsher, but do they amount to a "caricature?" Again, Hillary is admittedly a feminist, and she did liken marriage to slavery, at least in a legal sense. It might be going too far to say she "encouraged" children to sue their parents, but granting them the legal right to do so where they didn't have that right before is sure to have that effect. Notice that Carlson's objectivity completely disappears with the parenthetical statement "She did no such thing." Notice also that Carlson doesn't bother to quote Hillary's words in order to support that statement or the statement that the Republicans had "seriously distorted" her writings. As with all Hillary defenders, we are to take her word for it.

The article remains partisan right down to its last line: "Perhaps it is time to admit that 'two for one' is a good deal."

The False Charge of Sexism

Running through Carlson's article is the implication that the attacks on Hillary are sexist: "Still, Mrs. Clinton would have done well at the outset to have conformed more to the traditional campaign rules for aspiring First Ladies: gaze like Nancy Reagan, soothe like Barbara Bush and look like Jacqueline Kennedy."

Such insinuations run through the words of most Hillary defenders. Ted Koppel, on the 18 August

"Nightline," said, "Let us not for a moment be confused into believing this is only a conservative Republican thing, this business of some people feeling threatened by smart, assertive, professional women. . . . Women who speak their minds in public are still swimming upstream in this country."

Donnie Radcliffe, in the 30 October *Washington Post*, said, "It hasn't been easy being the Woman in the Year of the Woman, everybody's favorite target for all that's dangerous about being independent, smart, impatient, articulate, outspoken, ambitious–and while she's at it, a three-fer: wife, mother, and successful corporate lawyer. By any standard, Hillary Clinton has been a handful for America to deal with."

Another example is a 12 October *New York Times* essay by Deborah Tannen, author of *You Just Don't Understand: Women and Men in Conversation*. The "Real Hillary Factor," Tannen says, is "the double bind that affects all successful or accomplished women." If they fit the stereotypes, they are not taken seriously; if they depart from the stereotypes, they are criticized as domineering. Tannen continues to say,

> It is reassuring that the Republican attempts to make Bill Clinton's wife into "Willary Horton" failed, but it is instructive that the attempt was made. It forced us to ask: By what logic could it be scary rather than comforting for a President's wife, who everyone knows will have his ear, to be unusually intelligent, knowledgeable and accomplished? And to the answer: By no logic at all.

Tannen is, of course, right about all this. Where she is wrong is in the idea that the Republicans had ever attacked Hillary for being intelligent, knowledgeable, and accomplished. What they had attacked her for were her liberal positions, and they attacked her precisely because they knew she had the intelligence, knowledge, and ambition to affect public policy accordingly. Tannen is concerned about women not being taken seriously; well, the Republicans had taken Hillary dead seriously and treated her as an equal to her husband, and still Tannen was complaining.

Tannen's complaint, like Carlson's, is not really with the Republicans. It is with the American people. Hillary's negative rating in the polls was 24 percent before the primaries had even ended and 30 percent by July, before the Republican National Convention. Notably, Hillary fared as poorly among women as she did among men, which pretty much eliminates sexism as the problem. If the Republicans did anything, they merely exploited a societal distaste for women who do not seem to balance their career ambition with family and femininity. Such views may be sexist and regressive, but, in America, people get to vote for whomever they want for whatever reason they choose–they do not lose the right to vote simply because they are too ignorant to see the glory of the feminist vision.

If most Americans accept the stereotypes that fit the Republican world view more than they do the stereotypes that fit the Democratic world view, it merely means that Republicans will be elected. Unless, that is, someone distorts Republican actions and paints them as being sexist when they are, in reality, being precisely the opposite.

As Carlson herself admits, Hillary virtually gave in to these sexist stereotypes in order to help her husband's campaign:

> While the Republicans were busy painting Hillary as an overly ambitious careerist, she seemed to be consciously modifying her style. In the past few months, she has softened her image (much to the dismay of some feminists),

> grinning and gripping like a mayor's wife and baking cookies to show she is not a harridan. She has even learned to stand at the back of the stage and look at Bill with a convincing imitation of the Nancy Reagan gaze.

In other words, Hillary and her handlers were attempting to reduce her negative impact by deceiving the public. Nothing had changed in her positions or her plans once in the White House, but she would *pretend* that they had. She would pretend to be a dutiful, supportive, vacuous political wife. Such blatant hypocrisy on the part of a Republican candidate would have drawn withering fire from the press. In this case, it remained silent.

Katherine Boo of the *Washington Monthly* suggested in May that we compare the soft treatment of Hillary to the nasty investigations of John Zaccaro, husband of 1984 Democratic vice-presidential nominee Geraldine Ferraro:

> We need to look closely at what Hillary Clinton's firm earns in state business. That's a principle easily grasped when the subject is Billy Carter or Armand D'Amato. But in our sympathy for the difficulties women face in the working world, we've allowed relevant questions about wives' careers to be silenced by social mores and public disclosure loopholes John Zaccaro would have cherished.

In other words, the American news industry, that bastion of feminism, was being sexist in its coverage.

Conflicts of Interest

Daniel Wattenberg, writing in the August *American Spectator*, gave a fairly accurate summation of Hillary's image problems:

> The image of Mrs. Clinton that has crystallized in the public consciousness is, of course, that of Lady MacBeth: consuming ambition, inflexibility of purpose, domination of a pliable husband, and an unsettling lack of tender human feeling, along with the affluent feminist's contempt for traditional female roles.
>
> Usually when a public figure develops a chronic image problem, it is the result of searching investigative reporting, leaks, revelations, scandal: Dan Quayle's National Guard service; John Tower's drinking and womanizing; Nancy Reagan's new china, borrowed designer gowns, and astrology. The surprising thing about Hillary's image problem is that it is self-generated. No one in the press has really scrutinized her twenty years of political activism in the far left border regions of the Democratic party. . . .
>
> Hillary Clinton is a self-detonating explosive. The condescending comments and snide innuendos that have landed her in such trouble . . . have been *volunteered.* "She seems so poised and intelligent," laments a Clinton advisor, "and yet she always seems to be one smart remark away from getting in trouble."

Wattenberg's comments touch on a possibility Hillary's defenders would never admit: Maybe it wasn't Hillary's gender or even her ambition to power that people didn't like; maybe it was *her.* Politics is the art of both compromise and tact, and Hillary displayed a talent for neither. This was nothing new for her: as the first-ever student commencement speaker at Wellesley in 1969, she had begun her speech by criticizing the remarks of Massachusetts senator Edward Brooke, who had spoken just before.

Hillary the Hostess

The first interview Hillary granted as First Lady was with the food editor of the *New York Times*, and the stipulation was made that no questions could be asked concerning her role in government. Thus, this venerable news organ carried a front-page story portraying Ms. Clinton as the model hostess, precisely the image her supporters said she should not be forced to cultivate. To follow up on this scintillating story, Hillary's social secretary appeared on all three morning talk shows. Clearly, Hillary the politician was playing both sides of the fence, claiming access to power but dropping into stereotypes when it would help her politically. But, then, she had been doing this ever since Bill's first campaign. And, every time she did, she acquiesced to those stereotypes and contradicted her supporters who insisted that women should be allowed to be whatever they want to be.

Chapter Seven

Truth in Advertising

In the 1992 election, the media for the first time decided that it would examine political advertising for accuracy. Newspapers around the country began printing "truth boxes" examining individual ads. CBS's analysis was called a "Campaign 92 Reality Check."

Such an analysis would seem to be a legitimate undertaking, a way to protect the public from deceptive advertising. Unfortunately, the idea that the American news media should serve as our guardians against lies and distortion is ludicrous. Many of the examinations presented by local newscasts and newspapers were well researched and balanced. Many presented by the national media were not.

Example #1: NBC

On Tuesday, 3 March, Lisa Myers of NBC reported on distortion in campaign ads. She began with the ads of Buchanan and Bush. The Bush ad shown concerned his new agenda for economic renewal. On a television screen, we see the words "The Bush Agenda: Strengthen Our Economy, Make America More Competitive." The narrator's voice says, "Now he has an agenda to strengthen our economy and make America more competitive in the world." The television screen shows Bush at his desk with the words "Change Welfare:

Make the Able-Bodied Work." "To change welfare," says the voice, "and make the able-bodied work." Suddenly a red bar bearing the word "Misleading" appears across the ad. "That's misleading," says Myers. "Here's why." We cut to Bob Greenstein, identified as a "welfare policy specialist," who says, "In the three years he's been president, he's not submitted a single significant proposal in the welfare reform area." But, the commercial doesn't say that Bush has a good record of welfare reform; it claims only that he now has a proposal included in his agenda for economic renewal. To say that the ad was misleading because he had not submitted earlier proposals was itself misleading.

Myers then shows us a second Bush commercial, in which Gen. P.X. Kelley blasts Buchanan for opposing Desert Storm. Buchanan's opposition to Desert Storm while a commentator on CNN is a matter of record. But, says Myers, the Buchanan campaign claims that Kelley himself may have opposed the operation. We then see Kelley himself strongly denying Buchanan's charge. And, if Kelley did not oppose the operation, how was the commercial misleading? Myers herself has shown us that Kelley was not being hypocritical, and, even if he was, no one denies that Buchanan opposed the operation.

"Now the Democrats," says Lisa Myers. But, she goes on to show only Paul Tsongas, and the comment shown from Tsongas is from a speech, not an advertisement. Amazingly, Myers was unable to find even a single incident of distortion in Clinton's advertising. In case you're keeping score, that's two examples of supposed distortion by Bush—both of them unfair—and none by Clinton.

Example #2: The *Los Angeles Times*

One supposed example of Bush's "negative campaigning" during the 1988 campaign was his focus on the pollution in Boston Harbor as a way to attack Michael Dukakis's environmental record. But, in August 1992, a program called "Danger at the Beach," produced by the National Audubon Society and broadcast on PBS, confirmed that Bush's charges had been correct.

About the same time, the *Los Angeles Times* reported on a much smaller pollution problem in Arkansas. It seems that chicken processor Tyson Foods—whose owners were long-time financial supporters of Clinton—had polluted 150 miles of streams and lakes while Clinton had done nothing. Oddly, the same story expressed surprise that the Bush campaign was considering filming a commercial there. They would be disappointed, said the *Times*, because the state's main rivers and lakes were "largely clean."

Example #3: Bush's Tax Commercial

In early October, the Bush campaign began running what was undoubtedly its most effective television commercial. The ad showed a series of real people, their names and occupations given in subtitles. Then, fading in below that, was the amount of additional taxes they would pay under Clinton's economic plan. The point was that, despite his claims to the contrary, Clinton would have to raise taxes on the middle class to raise the revenue that his plan called for. Not only the Republicans, but many economists and other commentators had pointed this out before. Because Clinton was campaigning so strongly on the economy, this was a damaging charge.

The Clinton campaign showed its efficiency once again, and once again the media blatantly assisted it. They immediately began calling reporters around the country, insisting that the figures used by the Bush campaign were faulty and that this was another example of "negative advertising."

The result was unforgiveable. All three networks and most major newspapers did critiques on the ad. For CBS and the *Wall Street Journal*, this would be the only ad they would critique in the entire campaign, and they did so at the express request of the Clinton campaign. These organizations had been less aggressive back in August when Clinton had run an ad claiming that he moved seventeen thousand people off welfare in Arkansas but failing to mention how many had moved onto welfare in that time.

USA Today's analysis of the ad stated that "the ad requires a leap of faith to assume Clinton will raise taxes on the middle class—after he's spent part of the campaign talking about cutting taxes for the middle class—even if all his numbers do not add up." For anyone familiar with Bill Clinton's record, it would take a "leap of faith" to believe otherwise.

Example #4: Christian Action Network Commercials

In October, the Christian Action Network produced a thirty second commercial documenting the Clinton-Gore ticket's support for gay rights. The commercial simply reported the ticket's position on such issues as gays in the military, and material supporting the claims was supplied to broadcasters. Nevertheless, CNN, Fox, and stations owned by the three networks all refused to run the ad.

Example #5: *Time's* Lawsuit

It is common practice for candidates to reproduce newspaper headlines in their campaign commercials—just look at your next local and state election. During the primaries, the Clinton campaign quoted extensively a *Time* magazine news essay concerning the difference between Clinton's and Tsongas's economic philosophies. The ad misquoted the essay to suggest that Tsongas was practically an advocate of Reaganomics, yet *Time* magazine made no objection. But, in October, when a Bush campaign ad reproduced the *Time* cover that carried the headline, "Why Voters Don't Trust Bill Clinton," the magazine took the unprecedented step of suing the Bush campaign.

Tom Rosensteil suggests that the cover was "irresponsible" in the first place and that *Time* was suing Bush in an effort to "repair its reputation." But, it should be noted that *Time* is owned by Time Warner, which underwrote the Democratic National Convention. Time Warner could escape charges of partisanship only if it were pursuing the suit out of principle. Winning this suit would set a legal precedent which would have a profound impact on campaign law and practice. After the election was lost, however, *Time* dropped the suit, demonstrating that it had not really been concerned about the principle of copyright infringement after all.

Example #6: NBC

The evaluation of candidate veracity went beyond paid advertising to include general campaign statements. On 26 September, NBC's Garrick Utley analyzed President Bush's statement that Clinton had raised Arkansas sales taxes 33 percent. "Wrong!" said Utley. "In fact, sales tax in Arkansas went up just one and one-fourth percent, from three percent to four and one-fourth percent." Perhaps journalism school should include remedial math because this *is* an increase of 33 percent.

Example #7: NBC Again

The month before, on 27 August, NBC's John Cochran ran footage of a speech by Bush in which he claimed that Clinton's economic plan included "the largest tax increase in history—$150 billion." The word

"WRONG" appeared over Bush's face in red. "Wrong," said Cochran. "In 1982, Ronald Reagan and his vice-president, George Bush, presided over the largest projected tax increase in history–$152 billion." But, as the Media Research Center pointed out in the September issue of *Media Watch*, Clinton's stated figure of $150 billion did not include funding for specific Clinton proposals such as job training and health care. "Even if Cochran were correct," said *Media Watch*, "the same reporters who deplore painting Clinton as a tax-and-spend liberal are defending Clinton by saying he's only proposing the second largest tax increase in history."

Was the media biased in its efforts to act as truth police? According to the Center for Media and Public Affairs, more than half of the incidences in which reporters questioned campaign statements dealt with Bush, while Clinton and Perot were evenly split at 24 percent each. Two-thirds of the campaign ads scrutinized were Bush ads, while only 14 percent were Clinton's. Comments about Bush ads were 83 percent negative. And, while George Bush entered and left this campaign with a reputation for negative advertising, the fact is that in the entire campaign he ran only one more attack ad than did Clinton.

Clinton's Flip-Flops

As we've seen, the media truth squads analyzed campaign rhetoric as well as campaign commercials. But, again, Bush's comments received more attention than did Clinton's. On 27 September, the conservative *Washington Times* published a news analysis entitled, "Clinton's Flip-Flops Speak Volumes." This article included a list of Clinton self-reversals, few of which were reported by other media.

On federal funding of abortions, Clinton was quoted by the Associated Press on 1 October 1991:

"There's a big difference between being pro-choice and being for spending tax dollars for any kind of abortion. I don't think that's appropriate." But, a Clinton for President issues paper on women says, "Clinton's innovative and comprehensive health care plan would cover pregnancy-related medical procedures, including abortions."

On a litmus test for picking federal judges, Clinton told Bill Moyers in a 9 July interview, "It is [a litmus test] and it makes me uncomfortable, [but] I would want the first judge I appointed to believe in the right to privacy and the right to choose." Later, in another television interview, he said, "I have said that I would do my best, in the next appointment of the Supreme Court, to appoint someone who believes in the general rule of *Roe v. Wade*. That does not mean–I have no intention of giving somebody a test. . . ." Then, in a campaign speech just before the election, when his victory seemed assured, he said, "I will only appoint a prochoice justice to the Supreme Court."

On the Persian Gulf War, Clinton told the *Pine Bluff Commercial* on 15 January 1991, "I agree with the arguments of the people in the minority on the [congressional] resolution–that we should give sanctions more time and maybe even explore a full-scale embargo . . . before we go to war." But, in the 23 March issue of *U.S. News & World Report*, he is quoted as saying, "I supported the Persian Gulf war because I thought it was right and in our national interest."

On a middle-class tax cut, Clinton said in a Democratic primary debate on 19 January, "I want to make it very clear that this middle-class tax cut, in my view, is central to any attempt we're going to make to have a short-term economic strategy and a long-term fairness strategy, which is part of getting this country going again." In one of his New Hampshire television commercials, he said, "I've offered a comprehensive plan to get our economy moving again. . . . It starts with a tax cut for the middle class." But, on ABC's "Good Morning America" on 6 June, he said, "But to say that this middle-class tax cut . . . is the center of anybody's econom[ic] package is wrong." According to a 3 June United Press International wire, "Arkansas Gov. Bill Clinton, a day after capturing the Democratic presidential nomination, said the only way for the federal government to overcome the deficit is with 'a massive tax increase.' Once the middle class tax cut had served its political purpose, Clinton largely quit talking about it."

On a health care payroll tax, the Clinton for President issues paper states, "We don't need to lead with a tax increase that asks hard-working people who already pay too much for health care to pay even more. . . ." But, on 12 August, Clinton told the editorial board of *USA Today*, "There will be a buy-in tax, which they can call a payroll tax."

On tougher mileage standards for American automobiles, Clinton promised in a speech to environmentalists at Drexel University in April that he would sponsor legislation to "accelerate our progress toward fuel-efficient cars" by requiring an average of "40 MPG by the year 2000, 45 MPG by 2020." But, in a speech to the Detroit Economic Club in August, he told car makers, "I think we should be very flexible about imposing standards on the overall fleet as opposed to different sized vehicles. I don't think it's fair to impose a burden on an American fleet that has bigger cars in it than foreign competitors do."

There are, of course, many other examples of Clinton flip-flops. On 26 September 1986, Governor Clinton said in a letter to the Arkansas Right to Life, "I am opposed to abortion and to the government funding of abortions. We should not spend state funds on abortion because so many people believe abortion is wrong." In an October 1991 campaign interview, Clinton said, "There's a big difference between being prochoice and being for spending tax dollars for any kind of abortion. I don't think that's right." But, in a campaign letter dated 1 July 1992, he states:

> I have never wavered in my support of *Roe v. Wade.*
>
> Over the course of this campaign, I have repeatedly called for national health insurance which would cover the cost of pregnancy-related medical procedures including abortion. In Arkansas, I have fought against mandatory waiting periods and parental and spousal consent laws.
>
> If elected President, I will sign the Freedom of Choice Act to secure the right to choose. . . .

This second letter is probably correct—Bill Clinton has been prochoice throughout his public life. This makes his 1986 letter a blatant lie.

On the other hand, Al Gore, Jr. opposed federal funding for abortion while in the Senate but changed his position once he was on Clinton's ticket. Gore's flip-flop, like Clinton's lies, received little or no press.

The media did, of course, refer to Clinton as "Slick Willie" (a nickname he had earned early in his political career in Arkansas), and they did attack him for his waffling early in the campaign. But, as Clinton became first the nominee and then the probable victor, the media's contempt for his lying evaporated. The "Slick Willie" moniker disappeared, and the same media that accused George Bush of distortion even when he was telling the truth failed to challenge Bill Clinton when he lied outright.

Truth in Reporting: Clinton's Real Record

If the media were so concerned about truth in advertising and truth in campaigning, shouldn't they be equally concerned about truth in reporting? So far in this book, we've seen many examples of the media's failure to adequately report the facts of various well-known issues. What is perhaps more frightening is the media's ability to sweep other issues completely under the rug. In every case below, efforts were made by various parties to inform the mainstream media about something in Bill Clinton's record that would have a bearing on his ability to lead America. Notice that none of these were reported adequately, if at all.

Clinton's pro-death penalty stance was hailed by the press as the surest indication that he was a "new Democrat." But, in his first term in office as governor of Arkansas, he commuted the life sentences of forty-four prisoners, one of whom murdered again.

During his 1990 reelection campaign, Bill Clinton was asked, "Will you guarantee all of us that if re-elected there is absolutely, positively no way that you will run for any other political office, and that you will serve your term in full?"

"You bet," Clinton replied. "I told you when I announced for governor, I intend to run and that's what I'm going to do. I'm going to serve four years. I made that decision when I decided to run. . . . I'm being considered for the candidate for governor. That's the job I want. That's the job I'll do the next four years."

Coming less than a year before his presidential campaign began, these remarks can hardly be excused on the grounds that circumstances changed. In fact, Clinton had planned to run for president in 1988 and had even called a press conferencc to announcc his candidacy. But, according to Gail Sheehy, he and Hillary had a discussion just before the press conference about his so-called zipper problem. With so many rumors flying around, including the rumor of Gennifer Flowers, they decided the time wasn't right. Clearly, Clinton was poised for a run in 1992.

One of Governor Clinton's proudest achievements is the Governor's School, a summer program that attracts the best and brightest of Arkansas high school students. The Arkansas Department of Education says that the purpose of this residential program is "to provide gifted students a challenging opportunity to experience a variety of 20th century theories for the interpretation of facts. The emphasis of the school is on conceptual or abstract intelligence in contrast to practical or concrete intelligence." Does that suggest a secular humanist agenda to you? It should. The curriculum includes films and reading that promote the acceptability of homosexuality as an alternative lifestyle. Some students say the school taught them New Age beliefs. Eddie Madden, in a review of the school, says that it teaches deconstructionist literary theory, that a course on women states Christianity to be "anti-woman and anti-sexuality," and that lecturers have included Emily Culpepper, a self-described "free-thinking witch," representatives of People for the Ethical Treatment of Animals, and Sarah Weddington, Jane Roe's attorney in *Roe v. Wade*.

Bruce Haggard, director of the school, when asked why the school did not offer a variety of balancing views, said, "Many of Arkansas's brightest young minds were being held back by religious, conservative, overbearing training at home, and this is our first shot at them."

One student, apparently devastated by the school's undermining of his moral and philosophical belief system, committed suicide soon after returning home. According to *World* magazine:

> his mother found disturbing entries in a journal he kept during and after the school session. "The first entry in his journal was about what a super mom I was. Within three weeks, his entry was about how materialistic I was," she said. "After he came back from the Governor's School, his best friend was no longer his best friend. He had been best friends with her since second grade."

Education is an issue that elicits positive responses from voters these days, and the Governor's School would be an obvious sign of Clinton's commitment to educational excellence. Why, then, did his campaign not tout it? More importantly, why did the media never mention it? Could it be because the nature of the school would destroy their image of him as a moderate and a "new Democrat"?

When former Tennessee governor Lamar Alexander, a Republican, was nominated for secretary of education under Bush, the media gave a great deal of attention to a business in which Alexander had made a great deal of money. The press suggested that his profit constituted a conflict of interest, although such a conflict was never substantiated. Amazingly, this same media could discover no conflicts of interest in the entire twelve-year tenure of Gov. Bill Clinton. Was Clinton so honest in office?

First, there is the fact that Clinton's half-brother Roger was convicted for possession of and conspiracy to distribute cocaine but received only a two-year sentence of which he served only one year. The media did not mention this, although they did report that Bill Clinton had been strong enough of a leader to order the sting operation even though he knew it would entrap his brother.

More significantly, there is the case of investment banker Dan Lasater, a heavy financial backer of Bill

Clinton. Lasater was Roger Clinton's employer and his cocaine supplier. In May 1985, Lasater's firm received $750,000 in commissions for handling the sale of state bonds. Lasater was later convicted of cocaine charges himself, but one week after Clinton was reelected for his fifth term, Lasater received a full pardon from him.

In 1987, the Arkansas state legislature passed an ethics bill covering all elected officials. But, in a private drafting session, Clinton insisted that the bill be altered to apply only to legislators, removing himself from its provisions. The *New York Times*, to its credit, reported on this on 27 March, but the rest of the media failed to pick up on it and make it an issue.

Finally, there is the case of Bill Clinton's mother. In 1981, Virginia Dwire (now Virginia Kelly) was a nurse anesthetist at the Ouchita Memorial Hospital in Hot Springs. When a young girl was brought in for reconstructive surgery following an assault, Virginia was unable to properly administer the breathing tube, and the patient died. Members of the hospital staff complained to the medical examiner that Virginia Dwire had made mistakes before, but she was not reviewed. The medical examiner later claimed that he did not know Ms. Dwire was the mother of the governor, but an aide testifies that he had informed him of this. There is no solid evidence that Bill Clinton interceded to protect his mother in this case. More likely, it is one of those situations in which the matter is not pursued because of the people involved. The question is why the media failed to investigate the possibility of Clinton's involvement or to report on the possibility of favoritism in this case.

There are other such cases that went unreported or underreported in the press. Again, one must ask what would have happened to Clinton's narrow margin of victory in November had even one or two of these incidents been faithfully pursued by the media with even half the energy with which they pursued the all-important "Murphy Brown" story. Most likely, it would have meant that Bill Clinton would have had to wait at least four more years to be president.

Chapter Eight

So Much for Conventional Wisdom

Prior to the Republican National Convention, a lady named Ann Stone formed a group called Republicans for Choice. She and her group got publicity on every network and in most major newspapers. In one week, she appeared on "Larry King Live," "CBS This Morning," and "Face the Nation." All of these media outlets suggested or stated that she represented a "split" in the Republican party. By the time the convention arrived, reporters were repeatedly asking if the Republican party was enough of a "big tent" to accommodate a variety of views. The discussion by the platform committee on the abortion plank was reported as if a major battle were ensuing, yet the prochoice factions couldn't garner the few votes needed to force a floor debate. A favorite trick of the networks was to juxtapose such reports over pictures of prochoice protestors outside the convention hall, making it appear that these were Republicans protesting their own party.

How much of a following did Ann Stone and other Republicans for Choice really have in the party? Stone organized a "prochoice caravan" to go to the convention in Houston, garnering coverage on CNN and

CBS. Despite this publicity, when *New York Times* reporter Richard L. Berke checked out her Indianapolis stop, he found only a "sparse crowd." "The absence of public support for Ms. Stone's highly publicized effort so far does little to bolster the hopes of Republicans who favor abortion rights, and it tends to strengthen the arguments of anti-abortion Republicans who dismiss Ms. Stone as representing a noisy but small minority."

In other words, the Republican party was quite unified on the issue of abortion, yet throughout the convention the media continued to refer to it as one of the ways in which the party was split.

And, what about the Democratic National Convention? A request by prolife Pennsylvania governor Robert Casey to address the convention was turned down. Instead, Kathy Taylor was allowed to speak as an example of a prochoice Republican. Kathy Taylor had worked for Casey's opponent in Pennsylvania. NBC gave the story less than two minutes during its convention coverage. No network reported the censorship in its regular newscasts. When NBC's John Cochran asked the chair of the Arizona delegation, Janet Papolitano, if she thought this was wrong, she replied, "I think it was the right decision. The platform of this party is prochoice, and Governor Casey is not prochoice." Oddly, no one suggested that the Democratic party was not enough of a "big tent."

Even Tom Brokaw later admitted that Casey's plight should have gotten more attention. "During the course of the convention," he said, "it just kind of got lost in a lot of stuff. I think he should have gotten more attention for not getting attention."

But wait. There's more. Apparently many members of the Minnesota delegation were prolife, and they brought signs saying so. According to accounts by Nat Hentoff in the *Village Voice*, these delegates were assaulted, shoved out of the way so they would not be on camera, and told to get out of the Democratic party. One lady reported being screamed at, shoved, and having her shoulder wrenched when a heavy-set man tried to rip her sign from her hand. Another lady's arm was karate-chopped six times by a male delegate. A male delegate was told he would be "punched" if he tried to hold his sign up before the cameras. None of this made the news, even though a cameraman told the delegates he had gotten shots of the abuse.

These delegates told Hentoff that security guards were present but did nothing to protect them. "In the row in front of us," said one delegate, "there was Walter Mondale. He didn't say or do anything."

The characterization of the two parties' positions on abortion was slanted. The *Christian Science Monitor* said that the Republican platform contained a "total ban on abortion." Don Noel of the *Hartford Courant* said the platform called for a constitutional amendment "banning abortion under all circumstances." Adam Pertman of the *Boston Globe* said the platform called for a "constitutional ban to the procedure altogether." The *Washington Post*, the *Atlanta Journal*, and the *Los Angeles Times* published similar statements. Dan Rather said on the "CBS Evening News" that the party was "committed to a constitutional amendment to ban all abortions." John Chancellor said on the "NBC Nightly News" on 26 August that the Republicans had taken "the hardest possible" line against abortion. NBC's Tom Brokaw told President Bush in an interview that the platform advocated a total ban on abortion and asked if that didn't contradict his commitment to exceptions for such cases as rape and incest.

The platform does assert a right to life for the unborn child, and it does declare support for a human life amendment to the Constitution. But, it does not specifically say that such an amendment must outlaw abortion without exception. Some of the human rights amendments that have been proposed allow abortions for such cases as rape and incest. Besides, support for a constitutional amendment means support for a democratic decision made by the voters and state legislators—it does not mean that President Bush will attempt to use his executive power to force his views on America. Supporting the right to life for the unborn is, of course, precisely what we would expect a prolife party to do and it is perfectly mirrored by the Democratic party's plank supporting a woman's right to choose. To be fair, the same media outlets would have had to state that the Democratic platform called for "keeping abortion legal for any reason all the way up until the last day of pregnancy" because that is precisely what it did. Not a single reporter phrased it this way.

Other Democratic Splits

Abortion was not the only subject dividing the Democratic party that was not reported. Norman Segel of the New York Civil Liberties Union was quite upset that the homeless people had been rounded up and evicted from the vicinity of Madison Square Garden prior to the convention. ABC covered this on "Good Morning America"; the others did not.

One of the things that made Clinton a "new Democrat" was his support of the death penalty. But, not all delegates agreed with him, and, during a platform committee meeting, they tried to force a debate on the subject. When this was not allowed in the committee, they gathered enough signatures to force debate before the convention itself. Did the convention prove to be a "big tent" in which there is room for all voices? No, the Democratic National Committee *went to federal district court* to prevent the debate from taking place. No one in the media found this significant enough to publicize.

On opening night, there was contention because Jerry Brown was not being allowed to speak to the convention, or at least not during prime time hours. Every time chairman Ron Brown came to the podium, hundreds of delegates chanted, "Let Jerry speak." Some delegates were placing tape over their mouths to symbolize censorship. CBS covered this debate pretty well on the first night, although Ed Bradley said that it was not really a "problem," but just an "irritant." In any case, it was the strongest hint of disunity that the national media paid real attention to.

Perhaps the most significant rupture in the Democratic party was caused by the fact that the party's congressional leadership was tarnished by such recent scandals as the check-kiting habits at the House bank. Clinton wisely kept them out of sight, just as he did the former Democratic nominees Michael Dukakis and Walter Mondale. The networks cooperated with this effort, showing such non-entities only occasionally. Had the Republicans taken such steps, they would have been regaled by the press for "silencing" their members and playing blatant politics. No one in the media questioned the motives of such strong-arm tactics by the Democrats.

News Broadcasts During the Conventions: CBS

First, let's look at the "CBS Evening News" on the opening night of the Democratic National Convention. The broadcast opens with Eric Engberg's investigative piece on Floyd Brown's efforts to uncover information related to the suicide of Susann Coleman. The story lasted an extraordinary five minutes and forty-seven seconds. While Engberg makes it reasonably clear that Brown had no connection to the Bush campaign, the result is still a long piece that is negative for the party.

Next, Dan Rather gives a one minute, forty-two second overview of the convention that opened that afternoon. Nothing in this overview is negative for the Democrats. Mark Phillips then gives a two minute, forty-five second report on how the campaign is "playing in middle America," a collection of fairly innocuous comments by average people. After giving headlines of other stories, Rather turns to a four minute, thirty-four second interview with Jesse Jackson, which makes it clear that, while Jackson is not completely satisfied with the Clinton platform, he will support it.

Finally, Rather asks, "Are we going to have a fractured party and splintered convention as usual for the Democrats?" Richard Threlkeld, reporting from the convention floor, replies, "Two chances, Dan. Slim and none." He goes on for one minute and forty-three seconds listing the branches of the party that are lined up behind Clinton.

In all, CBS devoted sixteen minutes and thirty-one seconds to the campaign, almost half of which focused on the convention and the unity of the Democratic party. Of the total time, one-third was negative toward the Republicans, while nothing was negative toward the Democrats.

Now let's look at the "CBS Evening News" the opening night of the Republican convention. Other than two stories on foreign affairs, the entire show focuses on the campaign. The first story is an overview of the first day of the convention by Susan Spencer. After an initial shot of Bush entering the convention for what Spencer calls the "fight of his political life," she turns immediately to the abortion controversy, showing demonstrations on the street and some delegates holding up prochoice banners. Yet, Spencer reports that "the votes weren't there to even force debate."

"And there was another flurry of sleaze today," Spencer says. "Campaign chairman Bob Masbacher quoted as saying [*sic*] that questions about Gov. Clinton's marital fidelity 'should be one of the yardsticks' by which voters judge Clinton. Another Bush supporter called Clinton a 'skirt-chaser' in a speech yesterday." Spencer doesn't seem to realize that a comment made yesterday can not be part of a flurry that occurred "today." Yesterday, the convention had not yet begun, and Spencer gives no indication that the "Bush supporter" who made the skirt-chaser comment held any official position in the campaign or was even a delegate to the convention.

Nevertheless, she and others use the comment to attack Bush. "All of which," Spencer continues, "forced Mr. Bush to deny that he is privately encouraging any of this." We cut to a sound bite from a CNN interview with Bush in which he protests that he cannot control everything people say. Spencer then tells us that the Bush campaign has apologized to Clinton, and we are then treated to a comment from Clinton himself: "When he said in February this wouldn't be part of the campaign . . . there's been so many times when he said one thing and had his people do something else that I can't keep up with it."

Clinton here is explicitly accusing the president of lying, yet he offers no evidence to support his claim. The media which demanded absolute proof about the moral issue of Clinton's infidelity allowed him to make totally unsubstantiated claims about the moral issue of whether or not Bush is playing dirty politics and lying about it.

Finally, Bush gets a few seconds of positive coverage, but it doesn't come from Spencer. It comes only from a Bush sound bite from a speech to a veteran's convention. Spencer then closes with a fifteen second wrap-up concerning the question of what Bush will talk about at the convention.

At this point, the "CBS Evening News" has devoted two minutes and thirty-three seconds to the convention. Of that, one minute and thirty-seven seconds has been negative toward Bush, forty-one seconds has been positive, and fifteen seconds has been neutral. But, it gets worse.

The second story is a well-produced three minute, twelve second report on the effect of foreign policy on the election. The theme of the story is that, since foreign policy is Bush's strength, the end of the cold war hurts his chances at reelection. Today, we are told, the ringing of the White House phone late at night might just as likely concern south central Los Angeles or some other internal problem. The gist of this report is that, because the world has changed, Clinton's weakness in foreign policy will not prevent him from being as good a president as Bush. This is contradicted by the fact that the only reports on the "CBS Evening News" that night, other than convention coverage, concerned Bosnia and Somalia. In reality, of course, foreign problems became an albatross around the neck of the Clinton administration in its first year.

It is the last two stories that destroy any idea of objectivity by CBS. First, there is a three minute live interview with Clinton himself in which he is allowed to talk at one point for an amazing one minute and thirty-eight seconds, a length of time simply unheard of in contemporary newscasts. In the entire newscast on the opening night of the Republican National Convention, Clinton spoke for two minutes and fifty-seven seconds, while Bush spoke only a total of forty-five seconds, and part of this was spent defending himself. On the opening night of the Democratic convention, "CBS Evening News" had not given George Bush one second.

Finally, the "Eye on America" segment revisits the town where Ronald Reagan's "Morning in America" commercial had been filmed in 1984. Dan Rather introduces the segment with Reagan's classic line, "Are you better off now than you were four years ago?" (Rather, like Susan Spencer, seems to have a problem with the concept of time. The commercial had been filmed eight years before, not four. Besides, it was a Reagan campaign ad, not a Bush ad.) The two minute and fifty second report by John Blackstone insinuates throughout that the California town in which the commercial had been filmed is in terrible shape and has turned Democrat. He closes, for example, by saying, "Frustration and depression didn't seem to have a place in Cataluma eight years ago, but this year those emotions promise to shape much of the vote in a town where it's no longer morning in America."

Did the story really support this conclusion? No statistics were given concerning the local economy, employment, or poverty. It was stated that the factory shown in the commercial had lost four hundred jobs over eight years, but the report admitted that the factory isn't in Cataluma. Besides, no details were given as to why these jobs were lost and whether they were lost under Reagan or Bush. Two of the people who had been in the commercial said they would vote for Clinton, but two others said they would vote for Bush.

In all, the "CBS Evening News" devoted eleven minutes and thirty-five seconds to the campaign that night. Of this, ten minutes and thirty-nine seconds were negative against Bush or positive toward Clinton. Only forty-one seconds were positive for Bush, and nothing was negative toward Clinton. Only two minutes and thirty-three seconds of the entire newscast concerned the convention itself, and one minute and thirty-seven seconds of that was negative. This is before actual network coverage of the convention had even begun.

Republican Convention Coverage: PBS and NBC

NBC and PBS combined coverage this year. On Monday, 17 August, an unsmiling Maria Shriver asked Republican spokesman Craig Fuller about family values. "Craig, we were talking earlier about family values; that is the theme here today. A lot of people are saying that the Republicans by saying that . . . are really excluding everybody who doesn't fit into the traditional nuclear family, the Ozzie and Harriet image." Although this wasn't actually a question, Fuller went on to answer it pretty well. But, Shriver wasn't through yet.

"But people also want to know where in this image are people who are single mothers, who are black, people who are on welfare, who are homosexuals. They don't seem to be included in these family values."

"Well, I hope they don't feel excluded at all, because that's not our message. . . ."

"But they do," Shriver interrupted.

MacNeil and Lehrer then turned to a panel of three Republicans for their views. Robin MacNeil asked Rep. Marge Roukema of New Jersey, "In this year, when so many people are unhappy for economic reasons, is it good politics to give what may be negative signals to gays, feminists, black single mothers on welfare, prochoice women. . . ?" Like Shriver, MacNeil characterizes the Republican position as excluding blacks and people on welfare, something that no Republican had said. Representative Roukema said that she was "astonished" at the introduction here. She pointed out, for example, that welfare reform in New Jersey had been a bipartisan effort led by a black Democratic senator. Clinton had, in fact, talked about welfare reform in his campaign. No one had called him racist or exclusionary for doing so.

Bruce Herschensohn, a Republican senatorial candidate in California, spent his entire time blasting the media:

> I was pretty upset when I saw the analysis at the beginning of the show by John [Cochran] and Andrea [Mitchell]. The one at the Republican convention, the one at the Democratic convention, and when there was discussion of the Republican convention it was pretty negative stuff, they really had to be defensive about this. There was the word "racial," as if there were racial overtones, but when it came to the analysis of the Democrat convention, it was just fine. I have seen a great deal of this, not just lately, but through decades, but I've seen it regarding this convention. I'll be out on the floor talking to other delegates and the mood has just been terrific, really been up. Then I'll get an interview by someone in the media, and they're worried, they're scowling about what this all means, about what the covert reasoning is behind this particular platform position or this one. When, in fact, when you just walk among the delegates here, I think you're going to find a terrific amount of unity.

On Tuesday night, Shriver spoke with the two California men who were running against Diane Fienstein and Barbara Boxer in the senatorial races. "Both of you are campaigning in the year that is called the year of the woman; you're campaigning against two very visible women. How difficult has that been for you to compete against that? . . . Voters do see women as agents of change and they're asking for change. They don't see guys like you."

Bruce Herschensohn rightly replied, "You know . . . when you say something like that to me, that's sexist, and it's prejudiced and it's biased. I don't care about anyone in politics' gender. I care about what they think about issues and policies. Why do you repeat phrases, Maria, that are really sexist in nature?"

What the reporters, anchors, and commentators did at the Republican National Convention was to phrase their questions and comments from the viewpoint of the Democrats. According to the Media Research Center, for example, Democrats in 1988 had been forced to answer forty-nine Republican-agenda questions at their convention, while Republicans had been forced to answer 128 Democrat-inspired questions at theirs. By asking their questions this way, these reporters brought the Democratic rhetoric wholesale into the Republican National Convention. In doing so, of course, they put the Republicans on the defensive throughout their own convention.

They did not, by contrast, do the same to the Democrats. Did Maria Shriver ask Bill Clinton if his party's platform didn't exclude those with traditional moral values? Did Peter Jennings ask Clinton if he wished to "distance" himself from the radical gay rights leaders who had spoken on the opening night? Did MacNeil and Lehrer suggest that all the talk about helping the disenfranchised was just "rhetoric" designed to get votes?

Tom Brokaw ran down the gender and ethnic make-up of the Republican convention compared to that of the Democratic convention. The Republican convention was, in Brokaw's words, "more white and more male" than the Democratic convention. There was some irony in this, since all six anchors and commentators rounded up by PBS and NBC were white males.

Coverage of the Republican National Convention: CBS

An unsmiling Connie Chung, standing with the California delegation, refers to the split on the abortion issue:

> But George Bush's forces *twisted* a lot of arms and succeeded today, this morning, and prevented, and turned off, any attempt to debate the abortion issue. What he did succeed in doing is, at the same time, possibly turning and haunting him later on, particularly with one group with which he's had problems before, and that's women. That's especially true, and can be true, here in California, the reason being that there are two very well-known Democratic women running for the senate, and they are both pro-abortion rights. Now they will have no problem pushing their position. What they will do is, voters will probably vote for them but are not likely to cross over to President Bush. There are also other problems in California, the economy, unemployment is up, it's 7.9 percent. The women and the men will be looking to President Bush to make some concrete statement about the economy. Now, you know he's going to have to hit a homerun here, Dan, but they say it's awfully hard to hit a homerun in the Astrodome. [Connie smiles at last.]

Reporting from the crowded floor of a noisy convention must be a difficult task, and, in this case, Chung's report is just coherent enough to make it clear that she is not saying anything positive about Bush. If Bush twisted any arms, he twisted a lot fewer than Clinton had done to present the appearance of a unified party. Bush's prolife position, according to Chung, will hurt him with women. But, surely she means prochoice women, because his position will help him with the millions of prolife women, or do they not count? Chung assumes that virtually all California women will vote for the two prochoice senatorial candidates just because they are women (which would, of course, be sexist of these voters), and they will therefore not vote for Bush. Of course, anyone who votes for liberal, prochoice candidates of either sex is unlikely to vote for Bush, anyway.

Coverage of the Republican National Convention: ABC

On the opening night of the convention, Jeff Greenfield had prepared a report on how divided the Republican party was. The party was in "disarray," he said, comparing it to the 1964 convention in which ultraconservatives seized power and nominated Barry Goldwater, sending moderates into Lyndon Johnson's camp.

The evidence presented for Greenfield's thesis was that the southern, pro-death penalty ticket of the Democrats threatened the Republicans' traditional stronghold, that the economy threatened to hurt Bush, and that the end of the cold war reduced the importance of Bush's strongest point. All this was true, but none of it either caused or resulted from a splintered party.

"The Republican party is openly divided as it has not been in years," Greenfield tells us. "Divided on abortion, divided on an economic program for the next four years, divided on the competence of its vice-presidency." But, how true was this? Although there were certainly some prochoice Republicans and some who wished Quayle jettisoned for a less tarnished nominee, there were not enough of either to put such issues in question. It is true that Bush had disappointed conservatives throughout his term and thus allowed his party's base to erode, but an erosion is not the same as a split. At no time in the convention was there a serious, public effort by conservatives to challenge Bush's nomination or agenda.

Greenfield goes on to say that a good speech could give Bush a boost. "Still, it is very unusual to come to a Republican convention and find so many Republicans thinking and acting the way we used to think about Democrats." What did Greenfield mean by this? Was he referring to the tendency of Democratic conventions to be fragmented? Did he mean that many Republicans at the convention held liberal views? Either way, his report solidified the image of a party in disarray, which simply did not match reality.

Coverage of the Democratic National Convention: CBS

Dan Rather, more than a third of the way through the first night, said: "And as this convention listens to the Democratic national chairman Ron Brown talk about how the Republicans' supply-side economics have failed and how the Republicans are race-baiters, that's what's happening up on the podium. Let's go outside. Let's go to . . . Richard Threlkeld who brings us up-to-date on what Governor Bill Clinton is doing." In other words, Ron Brown was attacking the Republicans—engaging in negative campaigning—yet there were no complaints from the media.

Sen. Bill Bradley said repeatedly in his speech that Bush "waffled and wiggled and wavered" and referred to Clarence Thomas as "another Supreme Court justice who's not the best we could have." Gov. Zell Miller of Georgia called George Bush "a timid man" and said that "for twelve dark years, the Republicans have dealt in cynicism and skepticism. They've mastered the art of division and diversion, and they have robbed us of our hope." Former representative Barbara Jordan said that Republican Supreme Court justices "burden liberty" rather than protecting it.

Did anyone call this "negative"? Here is Dan Rather's comment: "Barbara Jordan, the clean-up hitter of three. Senator Bill Bradley was the lead-off hitter, Governor Zell Miller of Georgia was the designated hitter, the middleman who hit hard at the Bush-Quayle ticket and also hit at least a little bit at Ross Perot." And, that was it.

Rather interviewed Gov. Ann Richards of Texas. He asked her if it bothered her that there were no women on the Democratic ticket. He later summarized her answer this way: "Governor Ann Richards said no woman was really fully qualified this time around." Now, stop and think what would have happened if this question had been asked of, say, George Bush, and he had replied that no woman was fully qualified.

Coverage of the Democratic Convention: NBC

Maria Shriver to Elizabeth Glaser, AIDS victim: "You placed the responsibility for the death of your daughter squarely on the feet of the Reagan administration. Do you believe they're responsible for that?"

Glaser: "I . . . I believe that they're responsible for not moving fast enough, and I'm sure that we've lost many, many lives because of that. I have never pointed a finger at any one individual. . . ."

Characterizing the Conventions: The Democrats

Throughout the conventions, the comments made, not only by commentators, but even by reporters, characterized the conventions in two different lights. Republican speeches were "negative" and Republican positions were "extreme" or "ultra-right wing," and the party was in "disarray." The Democratic party, on the other hand, was "unified," the candidates were "moderate," and the party platform was "mainstream."

According to the Media Research Center, Republican speeches were labeled as "negative" seventy times. Democratic speeches were never characterized as negative. During the 1988 Republican National Convention, the networks had called the party "conservative" 182 times. In 1992, the networks seldom referred to the Democrats as "liberal." In fact, reporters went out of the their way to ensure America that the Democratic party was now solidly in the mainstream.

CBS's Susan Spencer, reporting from the floor the first night of the Democratic convention, said, "Even liberal Democrats now . . . are willing to swallow the problems they have with such a conservative pair in hopes of winning."

CBS's Bob Schieffer just after that said, "Other than that [Jerry Brown's desire to speak], I must say, it's one of the most unified conventions I've seen in a long time." Surely, he means one of the most unified Democratic conventions he's seen in a long time–it would be harder to be more unified than the Republicans during the last three elections.

Dan Rather, on the "CBS Evening News" on 14 July, said, "Here at the convention, the delegates are moving quickly to rally around the middle-of-the-road platform of the Clinton-Gore ticket."

And Dan Rather, on the "CBS Evening News" on 13 July, during an interview with Jesse Jackson, said, "There isn't much difference now between the mainstream Democrat and the mainstream Republican."

Conservative columnist Cal Thomas, sitting in for John Sununu on "Crossfire" on 10 July, asked Clinton media advisor Frank Greer, "How can you pass off these guys—Clinton and Gore—as being moderates when they've been endorsed by every left-wing group that has endorsed every other Democrat since the days of George McGovern twenty years ago?" Greer answered that they "are well in the mainstream of American political thought." He added that those areas in which they are not mainstream are areas that most Americans don't care about. When Thomas pointed out that many people care about abortion, Greer stated that "being prochoice is being basically in the mainstream of political thought." Such an astonishing statement—one which merely wipes away the single most divisive issue facing Americans today—is either blatant politics on Greer's part, liberal intolerance of opposing ideas, or a demonstration of ignorance of American politics that should disqualify him from working as a campaign consultant.

When Thomas asked Greer how Clinton and Gore were more moderate than Michael Dukakis other than on the death penalty, Greer replied that Thomas was "all wrapped up in labels the American people don't care about." Pushed twice by Thomas to answer the question, Greer did not name a single way in which Clinton differed from Dukakis, yet he repeated once again that Clinton and Gore were "mainstream."

The problem is, of course, that support for abortion for any reason throughout pregnancy, gays in the military, state-imposed family leave, state-funded day care, and massive health care reform cannot be said to be anything but liberal. By calling the Democratic platform "mainstream," these reporters were merely repeating the ticket's campaign rhetoric.

Characterizing the Conventions: The Republicans

John Sununu, on CNN's "Crossfire" of 26 August, pointed out that the Republican platform of 1992 was the same as it had been in 1980, 1984, and 1988. In those elections, it had been voted for by more than 50 percent of the American people, yet reporters were referring to the current platform as "extreme."

CNN's panel, gathered to analyze the speeches of Ronald Reagan and Pat Buchanan, was uniformly composed of Republican-bashers. David Broder of the *Washington Post*, Jack Germond of the *Baltimore Evening Sun*, Gloria Borger of *U.S. News and World Report*, and even host Catherine Crier could be counted on to be hostile to the Republican message. Broder said, "There is no limit to how far this party will go to tip its hat to the far right."

NBC's "Today" show, on 25 August, had a panel made up of three reporters, all of whom were vocally anti-Bush. Bryant Gumble introduced the segment by characterizing the campaign as "nasty," and all three reporters stated that it had become nasty this early because George Bush was behind in the polls. None of them gave any examples of this nastiness.

Peter Jennings interviewed George Bush the day after the speeches, and seventeen of his forty-two questions dealt with the tone of the convention. Jennings repeated several comments by Buchanan and others and then asked Bush, "Do you buy that stuff?" Did Bush agree with those statements? Did these statements fit Bush's pledge to be "kinder and gentler"? "Do you want to put any distance between yourself and some of Mr. Buchanan's gay bashing?"

When Jennings finally got off the subject of the convention, his questions became no more positive. How did Bush respond to Clinton's allegations that the Republicans were using Hillary as a "Willie Horton-like issue"? What did Bush mean when he said he would do "anything it takes" to win the election? According to Tom Rosensteil, it was only a call from a former ABC executive now on Bush's staff that prompted the interview to be edited so that the finished product was more balanced.

Compare this to Dan Rather's interview with Al Gore during the first night of the Democratic National Convention. Rather asks what are certainly hardball questions, but he then fails to follow up when Gore clearly fails to answer them:

> **Rather:** Question: You and Governor Clinton are presenting yourselves as agents of change. Yet, you are a person who grew up in Washington, D.C. You've been in public life . . . how can you say you're an agent of change? You've been part of the Washington establishment almost since birth.
>
> **Gore:** Well, I–it's true that I grew up, part of my life, in Washington as well as part in Tennessee. But during the part of my life which has involved my service in the U.S. Senate and the Congress, I have fought against the failed policies of the Bush-Quayle administration. And this whole contest that we are beginning here, it is about the country's opportunity to reach out for a dramatic change. . . . [Gore goes on three or four sentences about his ticket being the "clear choice."]

Rather: Senator, speaking of choice, you say that you're prochoice. Governor Clinton says this is a prochoice ticket. However, our research says that you opposed federally funded abortions. How is that prochoice?

Gore: Well, number one, there ought to be no doubt about the central point. The prochoice ticket is the Clinton-Gore ticket. I have always supported a woman's right to choose. If you or any of your listeners are concerned about preserving a woman's right to choose, vote for the Clinton-Gore ticket.

Rather: Senator, Republicans say, and I'm quoting now, that you're the one who first brought up Willie Horton during the 1988 primaries. Question: Will that be your role this time, however you want to cloak it, basically a hit man, an attack or perhaps counterattack point man?

Gore: Well, with all due respect, I would like to correct what they told you. I never brought up Willie Horton's name, I didn't know his name or race. I brought up the issue of crime and the issue of furloughs. And then President Bush brought up Willie Horton and then we began to see these ads that put his visage on the screen and I thought that those ads from that independent group supporting Bush and Quayle were blatantly racist, very different from attempting to deal in a responsible way with the issue of crime.

Rather: Senator Gore, thanks for being with us. Good luck as the week goes along.

Gore here is being a skilled politician–avoiding the questions and turning them into opportunities to attack his opponents. Dan Rather is *not* being a skilled journalist, asking no follow-up questions and making no other attempt to force Gore to answer his questions. The moral: Hardball questions are easy if you don't have to catch them.

The characterizing of the Republican convention as negative was widespread.

Howard Fineman and Ann McDaniel, writing in the 17 August issue of *Newsweek*:

> While Bill Clinton motors through the heartland with a cheerful middle-of-the-road message, Bush is conspicuously stroking the party's conservative wing, echoing the cutting rhetoric of yore: anti-tax, anti-crime, anti-abortion. And he's using time-tested slime-and-distance tactics. . . . The question is whether this kind of campaign is too late, too openly to the right, too raw–or just too familiar–to work one more time.

Ed Bradley, responding to Dan Rather's question of whether election night polls showed that the conservative tone of the Republican convention had affected the outcome:

> Well, I don't have it in this survey, but my recollection of talking to people in an informal survey . . . [is that] there were a number of Republicans who said they felt let down by their convention . . . [and] that some of the positions of the religious right did not represent the way they felt. I think this is an issue that's going to affect the Republicans four years from now. . . .

Ed Bradley, just a few minutes earlier, stating that the conventions were not an important factor in the election: "We gave the voters a list of things to choose from, Dan, things that helped them make up their minds. I think in past years the conventions were very important. . . . This year they fell at the bottom of the list."

Tom Brokaw to Pat Robertson on election night: "There are many people in the Republican party who believe that the Republican National Convention in Houston, at which you played a prominent part, was simply too extreme, too strident in its positions, and they cite your speech and Pat Buchanan's speech, as well."

Katie Couric to George Bush on the 30 October "Today" show: "I think some moderate Republicans were put off by the tone at the convention. The Republicans relinquished too much time to what some term the radical religious right. Did you feel comfortable with the convention? Do you agree with the tone and content of Pat Buchanan's speech?"

Convention Disparities

According to studies conducted by the Media Research Center, Democrats were called moderate or conservative fifty-one times and liberal only thirty-eight during their convention. Republicans, on the other hand, were labeled conservative or equivalent ten times more than moderate. ABC alone used twelve liberal tags in New York, but more than thirty conservative tags in Houston.

No Democrat was ever called far left or hard left, but far right and hard right were used often for the Republicans. Reporters asked the Republicans 135 Democrat-agenda questions but asked the Democrats only thirty-eight Republican-agenda questions. Democrat-agenda questions asked of Republicans outnumbered their own agenda six-to-one.

Only five Republicans were involved in network coverage of the Republican convention, as compared to eighteen Democrats. These Republicans included David Gergen, who had been on Reagan's staff but who consistently thrashed the Republicans in his comments and later ended up on Clinton's staff. Another of these Republicans was George Will, a long-time critic of the policies of George Bush.

The Speeches: Pat Buchanan

The characterization of Buchanan's speech as "negative" began before he even gave it. CBS's Bob Schieffer said, "Those who have seen the speech say it is really filled with red meat for the conservatives; they call it a 'speech tartare.'" Dan Rather referred to it as Buchanan's "sushi rhetoric," whatever that means. "If Pat Buchanan sticks to the text of his speech tonight, which has already been circulated among the press, what [Republican National Committee chairman] Rich Bond had to say about Hillary Clinton [will seem like] what a Sunday school teacher might say compared to what Pat Buchanan will say about her."

Joe Klein of *Newsweek* commented, "It's a measure of George Bush's desperation that this guy is opening the convention for him." You see the contradiction in all this? The Republican party is supposedly split, with Bush having lost his traditional conservative base, yet here are conservatives Buchanan and Reagan opening the convention for him. Yet, this does not show there is no split; this is an "act of desperation."

Newsweek, after the election, referred to Buchanan's speech as a "hate speech." Here's how "CBS Evening News" handled it on 18 August 1992:

> **Susan Spencer:** Ex-challenger Pat Buchanan, who used to refer to "King George and Little Danny," endorsed them last night, blasting gay rights, abortion rights, and Hillary Clinton in the process.
>
> **Buchanan:** The agenda that Clinton and Clinton would impose on America, abortion on demand, a litmus test for the Supreme Court, homosexual rights, discrimination against religious schools. . . .

Spencer: The object of the ridicule dismissed it.

Clinton: It's what they know to do. Divide, use those wedges, personally attack. That's what they're good at, and that's what they know to do.

The story before this on CBS was on how bad the economy is. The story after was about how George Bush was losing the drug war. The last story in the broadcast reported that Bush was "failing to catch on with women."

Even David Gergen, who had served under Reagan, said Buchanan represents "the negative side of family values. . . . That's the bashing of gays, the bashing of feminism, the bashing of Hillary Clinton." But, gay rights leaders, feminist leaders, and Hillary Clinton have long been openly assailing the traditional concept of the American family. How can one be expected to defend that traditional concept without attacking those who are attacking it? Why was no one pointing out that the gay rights and feminist leaders were guilty of bashing the family?

Like those on the convention itself, the negative comments about Buchanan's speech gave the impression that all the news media were reading from the same cue card.

Lisa McRee on the 4 November "ABC World News Now": "Patrick Buchanan's speech was one of those speeches that not many people will ever forget. It divided the party and many moderates were frightened away by that. Patrick Buchanan is a very smart man. . . . I find it hard to believe that he didn't know what kind of effect his speech was going to have."

Newsweek reporter Eleanor Clift on the 7 November "McLaughlin Group": "I also want to say thank you, Pat, for pushing the president so far to the right that it made it a lot easier for the Democrats to capture the mandate of the middle class. . . . What he [Buchanan] did was make George Bush kowtow to the right more than he needed to. He overcorrected with that convention, which portrayed the Republican party as a party of homophobics, and antichoice, antiwomen, and everything else."

And, what had Pat Buchanan really said? First, let's look at the charge that he was guilty of gay-bashing. Here is everything Buchanan said about homosexuality and homosexual rights in his speech:

> When the Irish-Catholic governor of Pennsylvania asked to say a few words on behalf of the 25 million unborn children destroyed since *Roe v. Wade*, Bob Casey was told there was no room for him at the podium at Bill Clinton's convention, and no room at the inn. Yet a militant leader of the homosexual rights movement could rise at that same convention and say, "Bill Clinton and Al Gore represent the most prolesbian and progay ticket in history," and so they do. . . .
>
> Yes, we disagreed with President Bush, but we stand with him for the freedom to choose religious schools, and we stand with him against the amoral idea that gay and lesbian couples should have the same standing in law as married men and women.

And here is everything he said about Hillary Clinton:

> Elect me, and you get two for the price of one, Mr. Clinton says of his lawyer spouse. And what does Hillary believe? Well, Hillary believes that twelve-year-olds should have the right to sue their parents. And Hillary has compared marriage and the family as institutions to slavery

> and life on an Indian reservation. Well, speak for yourself, Hillary.
>
> This, my friends, this is radical feminism. The agenda that Clinton and Clinton would impose on America: abortion on demand, a litmus test for the Supreme Court, homosexual rights, discrimination against religious schools, women in combat units. That's change, all right. But that's not the kind of change America needs. It's not the kind of change American wants. And it's not the kind of change we can abide in a nation we still call "God's country."

Powerful stuff, no doubt about it. But, in a thirty-minute speech of about 2,200 words, Buchanan mentioned homosexuality in only three sentences, and, in one of those, he merely reported the words of a gay rights leader. His only other comment, that homosexuals should not have the same standing in law as heterosexuals, is one with which millions of Americans agree, as Clinton found out when he tried to let gays into the military.

Buchanan mentions Hillary Clinton by name in only one paragraph. He talks about her record in that paragraph, then talks about the agenda that she and her husband share in the next. He does not attack her personally, and he does not attack her for being a successful woman. Even if the two sentences concerning Hillary's record are distortions, this could hardly be said to be a Hillary-bashing speech.

In reality, it is Buchanan's speech that was distorted by the media. Columnist Charles Krauthammer, a former speech writer for Walter Mondale, said that Buchanan ended with "images of M-16s" held by American soldiers against their own people. But, the story Buchanan ended with concerned the bravery of two young soldiers in protecting an old folks home from a raging mob during the Los Angeles riots. "Greater love than this hath no man," he said, "than that he lay down his life for his friend. Here were nineteen-year-old boys, ready to lay down their lives to stop a mob from molesting old people they didn't even know." Is Krauthammer suggesting that these old people should not have been protected? Liberal columnists such as Krauthammer, Henry Grunwald, and Anna Quindlen said that Buchanan had "called for a religious war." What he had actually done, both at the convention and throughout his campaign, was to state that there was a religious war going on, not to call for one. "There is a religious war going on in this country," he said. "It is a cultural war as critical to the kind of nation we shall be as the cold war itself." In other words, those who believe in traditional values must defend those values against an advancing liberal vanguard—hardly new sentiments.

Was Pat Buchanan's speech hate-filled and divisive? So that you can decide for yourself, the complete transcript of Buchanan's speech can be found in Appendix D.

The Speeches: George Bush

In his speech, Bush stated that Governor Clinton had increased taxes and user fees in Arkansas 128 times. Liberal columnist and CNN "Crossfire" host Michael Kinsley immediately branded the claim "a lie of gemlike purity and distilled cynicism." The *Boston Globe* then ran a story claiming that an anonymous Bush administration official admitted that the figure was bogus and that the president knew it. Clinton and others went on to use this story as evidence that the president had deliberately lied. Oddly, conservative columnist George Will believed that Kinsley had demonstrated the claim to be "a tissue of falsehoods," even though Kinsley had offered no proof of that. The

Washington Post ran an editorial saying that those who repeat Bush's charge "know they are making a fraudulent argument."

Nevertheless, the stubborn charge wouldn't go away. Finally, the Clinton campaign did what reporters should have done–it examined the facts and issued a list of the tax hikes and fee increases under Clinton's watch. The total: 127. President Bush had been off by one. The *Washington Post*, on 6 September, published a story on the issue, but it didn't get around to stating the figure until the fifth paragraph, nor did it bother to apologize for its earlier charge that the president of the United States was a liar. Michael Kinsley, likewise, has never apologized.

A Theological Debate Erupts

"To make this revolution, we seek a New Covenant to repair the damaged bond between the American people and their government." So says the 1992 Democratic national platform, and so said Bill Clinton during the Democratic convention.

The term "new covenant" comes from the Holy Bible. In Genesis 9:9, the Lord establishes His covenant with Noah and his descendants, promising never again to flood the earth. Moses and his people carry the ark of the covenant with them throughout their wanderings. But, in Luke 22:20, during the Last Supper, Jesus Christ says, "This cup which is poured out for you is the new covenant in my blood." This "new covenant" is the salvation of grace that comes from the sacrifice of Jesus Christ for our sins. It signifies a new relationship between man and God, one in which man wins full and free salvation through a spiritual rebirth in which he gives up his old self in order to be "reborn" in Christ.

What does Bill Clinton mean when he applies the term to the relationship between the American people and their government? Intentionally or not, he places government in the place of God. In doing so, he fulfills the greatest fears of those who have decried secular humanism and its belief in the ability of man to solve his own problems, thereby discarding the concept of God as mere superstition that gets in the way of the progressive vision.

Perhaps Clinton did not mean it this way. But, in his acceptance speech to the convention, he misquoted Scripture again in a telling way. "Scripture says, 'Our eyes have not seen, nor our ears heard, what we can build.'" Scripture doesn't say this at all. First Corinthians 2:9 says, "Eye has not seen, nor ear heard . . . the things which God has prepared for those who love Him." Once again, Bill Clinton has substituted what man can do under his own power for what God can do for man. In an earlier day, this would be punishable as blasphemy. Instead, the Democratic convention cheered, as did the media that is usually so firm about the separation of church and state.

Clinton's speech was not the first at the convention to violate this constitutional wall of separation. The Reverend Jesse Jackson had managed to misquote Scripture even more profoundly, although with less purpose. To the cheers of the delegates, he had referred to Mary and Joseph as "a homeless couple" and to Mary as "a single mother." In reality, of course, Mary and Joseph were not homeless–they were, after all, traveling to pay their taxes. And, Mary was pregnant before marriage only due to some highly unusual circumstances. Jackson's designation of her as a "single mother" led one minister to muse, "Well, perhaps Rev. Jackson just doesn't know the Father."

Things were different when the Republicans spoke of God, even though they did so more accurately. After the convention, Bush mentioned that the Democrats had left three simple letters out of their platform, "G-O-D." The media went wild. Bush and his supporters were intolerant and exclusionary, they said. The ultra-liberal National Council of Churches issued an open letter to Bush saying that God did not play partisan politics and that it was inappropriate to bring His name into a campaign. They had sent no such letter to the Democrats, but then, the Democrats had managed not to utter God's name even when quoting Scripture which originally included His name. In any case, the letter was widely reprinted and reported as one more reprimand to the Bush campaign.

Conclusion

Just weeks before the Democratic National Convention, Bill Clinton had made himself a national punchline by claiming that "he didn't inhale" when trying marijuana in college. Three weeks before the campaign, he had an unfavorable rating of 40 percent and a favorable rating of only 16 percent. By the third day of the convention, his unfavorable rating had dropped to 24 percent and his favorable rating had risen to 29 percent.

Keeping in mind that this took place during a "dead" period, after the primaries and before the general election campaign, what made the difference? Part of the answer lies in the usual bounce resulting from the extra publicity provided by a convention. And, partial credit must go to the savvy positioning of the Clinton campaign. But, such a jump also indicates that the media were giving the Democratic ticket a free ride, asking few tough questions, accepting Democratic statements at face value, and even echoing Democratic campaign themes.

The media then reported repeatedly that George Bush did not get the expected bounce from his convention. What could the difference have been?

Political conventions are, of course, little more than publicity shows these days. The question, again, is not what the parties did, but how the media covered it. The Democratic party, as the networks reported, was trying to put on the show of a unified party, while the Republicans were trying to put on a show of dedication to traditional values. Objectively speaking, there is some truth and some falsehood in both these claims. The difference is that the media allowed the Democratic party to project the image it desired, while doing all they could to denounce the Republican image as false, cynical, and mere politics.

Chapter Nine

It's *Not* the Economy, Stupid!

The media's assessment of the economy throughout 1992 was the most blatant example of the media repeating the Democratic campaign message. Clinton had wisely decided to focus on the economy, even hanging a sign in his campaign headquarters that said "It's the economy, stupid!" (As George Will pointed out, this made Clinton the first presidential candidate to save his opponents the trouble of calling him stupid by doing so himself.) As Clinton hammered at this message, many journalists assisted him by echoing his claims even when they were exaggerated and by failing to report good news that might counter Clinton's strength.

What Was *Really* Happening with the Economy?

In reality, the economy grew at an annual rate of 3.9 percent during the third quarter–the sixth straight quarter of expansion. The 1990-91 recession was very shallow, and it was part of a worldwide slowdown that had affected the United States far less than most European countries. The news got better as the year went on. Retail sales climbed almost 1 percent in October, and first-time unemployment claims were down sharply.

Still, the Democrats repeatedly claimed that we were undergoing the "longest recession since the Great Depression." Under Ronald Reagan, according to William F. Buckley, Jr., the country had experienced the longest sustained economic boom since World War II, employed eighteen million more Americans, and increased the GNP by 32 percent. The slowdown under Bush was relative to the much larger economy created under Reagan. Even if growth had been slow coming out of the recession, it was still growth. The problem with the Great Depression had been its depth more than its length, yet the media allowed this distorted campaign rhetoric to go unchallenged.

In fact, all of the negativism was part of a coordinated campaign to discredit the Reagan years as a period of unbridled greed in which the rich got richer and the poor got poorer. As just one of many examples, Dan Rather had this to say on the 29 October "CBS Evening News": "Everyone knows the rich got richer in the 1980s. Now a new study shows how dramatic the change was. According to the Economic Policy Institute, more than half of America's new wealth went to the richest one-half of 1 percent of families. The bottom 60 percent of families saw no gain or got poorer."

What Rather failed to point out is that the Economic Policy Institute was a liberal organization founded by former advisors to the Dukakis campaign *and by current advisors to candidate Clinton.*

Bruce Morton, on CBS's "Eye on America" on 27 October, said, "60 percent of American families had their incomes decline during the 1980s." Susana Ramirez, in a commentary on the 13 November "ABC World News Now," went so far as to say, "In the past few years, I have watched as this country changed from the land of milk and honey that my parents willed me to a landscape of homeless and underprivileged reminiscent of the worst of the Third World."

There are, of course, many ways to manipulate economic figures. But, according to Census Bureau figures, real income increased during the Reagan years by 10.7 percent for the poorest 20 percent of Americans, and by 9.7 percent for the next poorest 20 percent. Every income level gained during the 1980s and, significantly, the disparity between the incomes of women and minorities and those of white males closed further in the eighties than in any other decade.

President Bush, appearing on the "Rush Limbaugh" show in October, protested the doom-and-gloom reporting. "A lot of people think we're in a deep recession in this country. The irony is we are growing and we've grown for five quarters." This would explain why Bush did not do a better job of responding to Clinton's comments about the economy–things were not bad enough to need defending, and Bush didn't realize until too late the extent of the lies perpetrated by the Clinton campaign and the media.

Example #1: NBC

A perfect example is the lead story on the "NBC Nightly News" on Sunday, 26 January. "President Bush prepares to give his State of the Union message," says Garrick Utley, "and Americans wonder what he will propose to get the economy moving." The story, called "Great Expectations," is cast by both Utley and correspondent Lisa Myers in political terms. "What he says could be crucial for his reelection campaign and for the way we live," Utley says in his introduction. "As part of the White House strategy to show a 'caring' George Bush," says correspondent Jamie Gangel over appropriate footage, "the President and Mrs. Bush went to a black church in Northern Virginia this morning. But with just two days left until his State of the

Union message, voters are waiting to see the substance behind Bush's promise to bring back the economy." Graphics then list the highlights of the proposals Bush is expected to make, proposals such as tax credits for first-time homebuyers.

This segues nicely into the kitchen of a young Virginia couple wishing to buy their first home. But, it seems the idea of a tax credit is not a full solution in the minds of this couple. "I would prefer seeing something happen to the economy that's long term that will help the economy overall," says the wife. "Quick fixes are great for now, but that's not going to help us in two years. . . ." We then jump to a man in Atlanta who claims to be a lifelong Republican and who wants to vote for Bush again. Unfortunately, he has recently lost his job. "It's not, 'What can I do for the country?'" he says of Bush, "but, 'What can I do to get reelected?'" Next is a lady who owns a child care center in Texas. Is she excited about these tax credits and other proposals? Why, no. "The peace dividend might actually hurt her business," says Gangel. It seems that many of this lady's clients are employees of General Dynamics, and if defense contracts are cut back, she will lose business. In other words, Bush hurts people if he offers tax credits paid for by defense cutbacks, and he hurts people if he doesn't. Amazingly, the combined resources of the NBC news machine were unable to come up with a single person out of 260 million Americans who actually *liked* the idea of a middle-class tax credit.

Example #2: *Time*

Another case in point is the October issue of *Time*. The cover story was entitled, "The Economy: Is There Light at the End of the Tunnel?" The first page of the article offered a large checklist of nine different "burdens that are weighing down the economy." In several cases the "burdens" could have been restated as positives. Even in the middle of a negative article, the magazine admitted that unemployment, interest rates, and inflation were low. But, the magazine turned even these facts into negatives. "Low inflation has almost completely removed the urgency to dash out and buy a house before the price goes up." Thus, low inflation becomes a burden to the housing industry and, thus, to the entire economy. On the third page of the article, the magazine admits that Ford and Chrysler now rank as the world's lowest-cost producers of automobiles.

Example #3: CBS

Now, let's look at the "CBS Evening News" on 18 August, during the Republican convention. New government figures showed housing starts down by 2 percent. Dan Rather led with the story, giving it two minutes and showing several housing contractors with tales of woe. But, the very next night, when government figures showed that the trade deficit had improved, Rather gave it a total of twenty seconds, two-thirds of the way through the newscast.

On 30 October, just four days before the election, Rather reports on housing sales: "The Commerce Department says sales of new homes fell 1 percent in September, the first outright drop in five months. For the first nine months of the year, sales are more than 20 percent above the same period of last year." This good news got a full fourteen seconds of air time, with the bad news of September leading.

Example #4: The *New York Post*

The bashing continued even after the election. The *New York Post* ran a front page cover headline that said, "Hey, Bill. George Cooked the Books." Columnist John Crudele claimed that Bush had kept two sets of books, one with optimistic economic news for the public, another showing the horrible truth. Offering no proof other than the word of an unnamed source, Crudele said that the administration had "purposefully tampered" with the figures. He insinuated that the government had withheld the third-quarter figures until after the election so that the Bush campaign would not be hurt by the bad news. In reality, of course, Bush would have been greatly aided by the revelation that unemployment had fallen to 7.4 percent.

The Bureau of Labor Statistics–a non-partisan agency which prides itself on its professionalism and objectivity–took the unusual step of sending a scathing letter to the *Post*. That didn't stop Larry King from asking Labor Secretary Lynn Martin about it on his show.

Studies of Media Bias

According to the Center for Media and Public Affairs, counting only the evening news broadcasts of the three networks, 1,083 stories on the economy aired in 1992, an average of one per network per day. Even with an ailing economy, one has to ask if there was actually *news* on this subject every day; that is, was there a change in the situation prompting daily coverage? No, there was only the desire to hammer at the negative image of the economic situation.

From July through September, 96 percent of sources interviewed on nightly newscasts characterized the economy negatively, 5 percent higher than average. During those three months, the economy grew 3.9 percent, the sixth straight quarter of growth.

The Media Research Center studied 2,531 stories on the economy from October 1990 to September 1992. "Economic coverage more than doubled during the [election year], with the monthly average jumping from 63 to 148 stories." More than 770 of these stories were on unemployment. The recession came in second with 534 stories. "Evaluations of America's economic condition were consistently negative. Of the 1,815 assessments of the overall economy and its major sectors, 91% were negative." In the quarter leading up to the election, this rose to 96 percent. In the month before the election, it rose to 98 percent. But, why, when the economy was actually improving during this time?

CBS, on 5 April 1991, was quoting a union worker as saying, "We're in a depression. We're not in a recession. There's no work. There's no jobs." On 4 August 1992, they were quoting economist Allan Sinai as saying, "We'll be lucky if we can keep our head above water."

Of economists quoted since the primaries, two-thirds opposed Clinton's plan, but five-sixths opposed Bush.

In a study by the Media Research Center of network stories from December 1991 to March 1992, "the word 'recession' was uttered by reporters 260 times, an average of more than twice a day." Of sources quoted, "96% agreed that the recovery would be weak or slow to develop."

Seventy-one percent of individuals profiled in economic reports had suffered economically. Sixty-two percent of business profiles were positive, but they were often framed as companies bucking the downward trend, such as ABC's 14 January look at a discount mall frequented by victims of the recession.

Just before the election, CBS ran a week-long series called "The Money Crunch: Making it in America." Dan Rather introduced it as "Surviving in the 90s." From the parent trap to the difficulty of saving for retirement, the series focused on a variety of economic problems in America. The series was cleverly disguised in a "consumer tips" format, but the timing of the series can hardly be coincidence.

The Center for Media and Public Affairs found other ways that the media catered to Clinton's economic agenda. In a study of news stories from November 1991 to April 1992, the center found that evaluations of America's health care system were 86 percent negative. Opinions on the adequacy of federal funding for health care were 100 percent negative. Clinton was running on a platform of universal health insurance.

During the same period, reports the center, "discussions of domestic policy outnumber foreign policy debates by a six-to-one ratio, and two-thirds of the domestic debate concerned economic issues. One in every five election stories has featured a discussion of the economy." Statements about the state of the economy were 92 percent negative. Seventy-nine percent of sources quoted said the nation faced troubled times. Ninety-seven percent of statements about Bush's tax policies were negative.

The natural response to this is that, if the economy is bad, then, of course, the news about it will be bad. But, the economy was not as bad as the media portrayed it, as is evidenced by the fact that negative characterization of the economic situation merely increased as the economy improved. The complete absence of dissenting voices was also suspicious.

A Man with a Plan

Clinton won much respect with this national economic strategy plan, "Putting People First," which he made available through a toll-free number and at local libraries across the country. As David Broder wrote in the *Washington Post*, the plan showed that Clinton was not just "another blow-dried politician with a smooth way of talking."

But, Robert Samuelson, also writing in the *Post*, did something that neither Broder nor most other reporters did: he actually looked at the plan and described it for his readers. Clinton's "Putting People First," he pointed out, was only twenty-two double-spaced pages long. "His claims that he will cut the deficit in half in four years are mostly bogus," Samuelson said. "His theory that 'investing in people' automatically leads to economic growth is largely wishful thinking. And the notion that he's being candid is nonsensical."

One flaw in Clinton's plan was easily detectable. "Putting People First" claims that Clinton's tax increase would affect "only the top 2%" of wage earners, which Clinton repeatedly said would include only those making $200,000 or more. Internal Revenue Service records show that those earning $200,000 or more make up only 0.7 percent of wage earners. The top 2 percent includes those making as little as $122,000, a figure which includes many two-job couples filing joint returns who had previously thought of themselves as middle class.

This glitch was significant because it meant that Clinton must either tax more people than he claimed or raise less revenue. Either way, his economic plan was seriously flawed. There were other problems as well, such as the plan's failure to take into account the nearly one million lost jobs that will result from Clinton's defense cuts.

The media, to its credit, did ask some hard questions about these discrepancies. But, they failed to hammer at it in the same way they hammered at the Reagan-Bush record and at the negative aspects of the current economic situation. They failed to make it "the issue" even though it was the main issue on which Clinton was running. By the time Clinton had become the nominee and the probable winner of the general election, the media moved squarely into Clinton's corner.

When Dan Quayle said in the vice-presidential debate that Clinton's tax plan would affect people earning as little as $36,000, the press leapt to Clinton's defense. "There are some factual things to clean up," said NBC's Tom Brokaw just after the debate. "When Dan Quayle said they would be raising taxes on people down to about $36,000, that's based on Bush campaign projections of the Clinton economic program." ABC's Jeff Greenfield said:

> The Bush campaign calculates that since Clinton could not possibly raise the money he needs to pay for his spending programs with his revenue proposals, he would have to impose a 36 percent tax rate on anyone making over $36,000 a year. Independent examination of this charge by, for example, press organizations, has found it, to say the least, misleading.

And, CNN's Brooks Jackson accused Quayle of "twisting" and "misstating" the facts.

But, as the Media Research Center points out, *USA Today* said on 18 February 1993, "Looks like Dan Quayle was right. Last year's vice-presidential debate . . . produced an accurate prediction from Quayle about the Clinton budget plan. . . . The final plan, according to Clinton officials, will hit those making $30,000 and above."

NBC correspondent Andrea Mitchell on the 20 October "Today" show:

> One of the best things about Bill Clinton's campaign, I think, has been that he has criticized George Bush's no-tax pledge, saying he would never take such a pledge. Well, last night he came awfully close. There are a lot of loopholes in his pledge, but he said he would never

> tax the middle class, and if things don't work out right, he still won't tax the middle class. I think that's one of the worst things I've heard from Bill Clinton.

Let's take this one from the top. First, Bill Clinton had not criticized Bush for *making* a no-tax pledge, but for *breaking* that pledge. This criticism suggested that Bill Clinton was against raising taxes, so reporters naturally asked him if he would take such a pledge, which he refused to do. Second, Clinton had indeed said that he would not tax the middle class, and that if things went wrong with his economic plan, he "still would not tax the middle class." Where in such a statement Mitchell is able to find "a lot of loopholes" is a mystery.

All of which illustrates the great irony of the 1992 election campaign. The most solid and successful attack on George Bush concerned his broken pledge not to raise taxes. America then went on to elect a man who clearly *would* raise taxes. Bush was also attacked on the grounds that he had possibly lied about his involvement in Iran-Contra. Those who attacked him were supporting a candidate who had lied about his draft record, who had been unfaithful to his wife, and whose campaign rhetoric showed a clear trail of duplicity.

Mitchell's comment leads one to believe that she, unlike most Americans, does not think a tax cut to be important. She is not the only one. Sam Donaldson, on "This Week with David Brinkley" on 21 February, had this to say:

> I would tell him [Clinton] . . . [to] get real on the energy taxes. That's the way we're going to go. Don't put seven cents on. To be effective, put fifty cents on. We are still undertaxed on energy by large quantities, and we can stand it.

> So let's not just ratchet it up year after year, because once a tax is in place, folks, it just increases. Let's do it now.

NBC commentator John Chancellor concurred on the 16 February "Nightly News," saying that we should follow the lead of other industrialized countries and institute "a broad-based tax on energy or consumption, preferably both." And, *Newsweek*'s Margaret Warner, on CNN's "Capital Gang" on 28 November, said, "I think it would be entirely to the good if it [improved growth] made him abandon this ridiculous middle-class tax cut. Because the fact is what Clinton needs even in the intermediate term is a global stimulus package." So, now we find that those who defended Clinton's pledges to cut taxes were not in agreement with those cuts in the first place.

Clinton's Economic Record

What didn't get covered adequately in all this economic reporting was Bill Clinton's own economic record while governor of Arkansas. A close analysis shows that Clinton lied throughout the campaign about his achievements in Arkansas.

For example, Clinton claimed that Arkansas had the forty-ninth lowest tax burden. But, according to the Media Research Center, this was measured not by percentage of income going to taxes, but by per capita tax payments. By this measure, Arkansas was indeed at the bottom of the scale, but only because its population was so poor that its tax revenues were low. When measured by percentage of income, Arkansas ranked somewhere in the middle.

Clinton claimed that "Arkansas now leads the nation in job growth." On the contrary, according to columnist Donald Lambro, "employment grew by only 13.4% during the 1980s under Mr. Clinton's administration, compared to 17.5% nationally and 22.8% in the state during the 1970s." Furthermore, he says, Arkansas ranked forty-sixth in job quality and last in worker safety programs and worker's compensation.

One Clinton campaign commercial claimed that Arkansas incomes "are rising at twice the national rate." But, according to Lambro, the state's actual growth rate was 11 percent lower than the national rate and almost 50 percent lower than the state's rate in the 1970s.

In this same commercial, Clinton also claimed that he had "moved 17,000 people off welfare" in Arkansas. "I have a plan to end welfare as we know it–to break the cycle of dependency. I know it can work. In my state, we've moved 17,000 people from welfare rolls to payrolls." But, according to the *Washington Times*, the number of people on welfare and food stamps had risen by 27 percent during Clinton's tenure. When confronted with this, Clinton spokesperson Dee Dee Myers said that the ad was referring to Clinton's Project Success, which had indeed moved 17,000 people off welfare. But, while Clinton's program helped 17,000 people off the welfare rolls, more than 80,000 moved onto them. Does this suggest an approach that would help cure America's welfare problem?

Was Clinton's image as a moderate "new Democrat" realistic? Not according to Christopher Georges of the *Washington Monthly*, who wrote:

> Thirty-nine of the 49 specific proposals in Clinton's national economic strategy are virtually identical to policies proposed in 1988 by Michael Dukakis. His education agenda is virtually identical to Mr. Dukakis's Stars and Stripes Plan, his National Apprenticeship plan was Mr. Dukakis's Job Start, and his Youth Opportunity

> Corps was Mr. Dukakis's Educational Excellence Mentors.
>
> Mr. Dukakis offered a detailed plan to invest in America's infrastructure, part of which he labeled the Fund to Rebuild America. Mr. Clinton gives us a Rebuild America plank, which reiterates almost all of Mr. Dukakis's planks. Point after point, the agendas match. . . . It should come as no surprise that Mr. Clinton would fill his agenda with reruns. After all, a number of his top domestic policy advisors are the very people who engineered Mr. Dukakis's agenda.

How Quickly Things Change

The election was held on 3 November. On 6 November, a headline in the *New York Times* read, "Growth in October Lifts Retailers' Hopes for Holiday Sales." Kenneth Gilpin, the writer, referred to a trend in sales gains "that began in August." On the same day, the *Times* reported that "new unemployment claims in late October fell to . . . the lowest in more than two years." On 13 November, the paper reported that "the number of Americans filing for jobless benefits fell to a two-year low in late October and remained under 400,000 for the sixth consecutive week." On 18 November, the *Times* reported on the increase in consumer spending during the third quarter. On 30 November, the *Times* headline read, "Is the Clinton Expansion Here? Rebound Seen, But a Slow One." But, this was a story about the economic statistics for the third quarter. Clinton was now getting credit for things that occurred before he was even elected.

As the Media Research Center reports, the media had some difficulty adjusting to the novelty of giving a positive spin to economic news. They point to two examples of contradictory statements.

First, in the 23 November issue of *Time*, John Greenwald wrote, "Most economists agree that the U.S. recovery is far weaker than the recent 2.7 GDP growth spurt indicates. . . ." Two weeks later, the same magazine declared, "Gross domestic product leaped up at an annual rate of 3.9 percent in the third quarter, returning total output of goods and services to the pre-recession pace of mid-1990. Strong increases were registered by consumer spending, business investment, orders for durable goods, sales of existing houses and consumer confidence. . . ."

Second, Peter Jennings, on ABC's "World News Tonight" on 27 October, said, "[The 2.7 percent rate] is more than economists had projected, but in many cases, less than meets the eye." The next night, he added, "The president may complain about the news media, but the economic growth figures which he is so pleased about are not definitive, according to a great many independent economic analysts." On 25 November, Jennings changed his tune without acknowledging his earlier inaccuracy: "Timing may not be everything, but it certainly is crucial in politics. Three weeks after President Bush lost the election, and several months after insisting the economy was on the verge of an outstanding recovery, President Bush finally got the numbers he was waiting for. The government reports today that the overall economy grew faster during the third quarter of this year than at any time since Mr. Bush became president, not by 2.7 percent as first estimated, but by 3.9 percent."

The consumer confidence index stood at 73.3 percent at the end of October. By the end of November, it had risen to 83.6 percent. Part of the reason was the growing optimism that a change in leadership usually brings. Another part is that the media—after two years of hammering on the negative aspects of our economy—suddenly changed their tune. The stories of the poor and unemployed became less frequent, and good economic news suddenly got top billing again. The war had been won, so it was safe to admit once again that America is the most affluent nation in the world.

Chapter Ten

Landslide!

On election night, it looked like a landslide for Clinton. ABC said Clinton had won 362 electoral votes to Bush's 80. By displaying this number well before the West Coast polls closed (in fact, with only 58 percent of precincts reporting), it obviously discouraged Bush supporters from bothering. ABC did have a board displaying the popular vote, which was much closer, but this board was placed to the side and shown only a few times the entire night.

By 10:00 P.M. EST, NBC had given 254 electoral votes to Clinton and only 54 to Bush. By morning, however, the gap had closed substantially. Bush ended up capturing 168 electoral votes, not just 54 or 80. But, it was too late. The media the next morning had already delivered their verdict.

On CBS's "This Morning," correspondent Randell Pinkston referred to "the Clinton landslide."

Bryant Gumble introduced the "Today" show with the words, "A landslide victory ushers in the Clinton era." When interviewed later in the show, Republican campaign chairman Rich Bond complained about this terminology, pointing out that Clinton received only three hundred thousand votes more than did Michael Dukakis.

USA Today's headline was the single word "Landslide." The paper's readers seemed puzzled by this. "How can anyone characterize Clinton's win as a landslide when nearly 60% of the voters did not vote for him?" wrote one. Another said, "With the new president-elect receiving only 43% of the popular vote, you have created a new definition for the word [landslide]."

Newsweek called Clinton a "landslide winner" and referred to his election as a "sweeping victory." All of this ignored the fact that Clinton beat Bush by only 5 percent of the popular vote.

The next night, ABC's Peter Jennings was nice enough to state that "the landslide was in the electoral votes." But, he added:

> The senate minority leader Bob Dole said this morning he didn't think Clinton had much of a mandate. "Take all the people," he said, "who voted for Bush and Perot, and you get 57 percent voting against Clinton." True. Take all those who voted for Perot and Clinton and you get 60 percent who voted against the president and for some kind of change.

A good point, but one which merely proves Dole's statement. A mere 3 percent difference in the number of those who oppose the two candidates can hardly give Clinton a "mandate."

Refuting the Terminology

The real problem with the term "mandate" is not its numerical inaccuracy, but its connotation. As Thomas Oliphant of the liberal *Boston Globe* pointed out, "it implies much more of a blessing than was actually conferred by a thoroughly fed-up electorate. It also implies that Tuesday night's verdict was much more of a referendum on Bill Clinton's ideas and political message than it in fact was." He suggests that Perot's good showing was partially the result of so many being tired of Bush but unwilling to vote for Clinton.

Grover Norquist, writing in the *American Spectator*, pointed out that Clinton got 3 percent fewer votes than Michael Dukakis had in 1988. Like many other observers, he pointed out that the conservatives who abandoned Bush did so because he had increased government spending and regulation, betraying Republican ideals and laying the foundation for Perot's popularity. The candidates with more conservative economic policies–Bush and Perot–together received 57 percent of the vote, much closer to a mandate than Clinton received.

The *National Review* asked how a mandate can be smaller than a majority. It pointed out that even Arkansas gave Clinton only 54 percent, and was one of only three states to give him 50 percent or more. In addition, the Democrats lost ten seats in the House of Representatives and gained only one in the Senate. The magazine went on to say:

> If the Democrats have no mandate from the voters, however, they enjoy a historic one from the media. E.J. Dionne, Jr. writes in the *Washington Post* that this election has "overturn[ed] the verdict reached in 1980." Somehow Mr. Clinton's 43% has retroactively nullified what amounts to three Reagan landslides. Mr. Reagan, of course, never won a media mandate. He now turns out to be beatable, provided he isn't on the ballot.

According to *USA Today*, none of the nation's fifty largest papers said George Bush's 1988 victory was a landslide.

Time's Assessment

After each election, *Time* magazine puts out a special election issue. The cover of the 16 November issue carried a photo of Clinton and trumpeted, "Mandate for Change." A blurb at the top of the table of contents said, "A broad coalition sweeps Bill Clinton into the U.S. presidency with a mandate for change." The title of the main story is "A Time for Courage." The subtitle is "If Clinton is to fulfill his mandate for change, he will have to be honest about uncomfortable truths and brave in making tough choices."

Now, let's look at *Time*'s election special of four years before. Where Clinton had won 370 electoral votes, thirty-two states, and 43 percent of the popular vote, in 1988 George Bush had won 426 electoral votes, forty states, and 54 percent of the popular vote. Did the cover of the 21 November 1988 issue trumpet the continuation of Reagan's mandate? No, the cover title was a bland "President-elect George Bush Savors His Victory." The blurb at the top of the table of contents begins positively, then gets in a dig at the end: "A decisive victory sets the stage for the Bush years, and the U.S. looks ahead to a leader who offers continuity more than vision." The title of the main story, "What to Expect," is followed by this flattering subtitle: "The outlook for the Bush years: Reaganism without ideology, persistence without brilliance–and serious trouble with Congress." The same magazine that referred to Clinton's victory as "sweeping" and "a mandate" had referred to Bush's victory as a "mini-landslide."

Newsweek had been a little more accurate in 1988. According to the text of its story, Bush's election was "very nearly a landslide." A graphic was nice enough to call it "A Blowout in the Electoral College," and the subtitle of one story did refer to Bush's "electoral landslide." But, accuracy doesn't always lead to fairness. *Newsweek*'s cover title on 21 November 1988 was "How Bush Won." The answer to that question, according to several articles inside, was that he used dirty tricks, distortion, and negative campaigning. The title of the main story, "The Tough Tasks Ahead," is following by this subtitle: "George Bush wins a decisive victory and a personal vindication, but no clear mandate. What kind of president will he be?" Bush did indeed have a clear mandate, of course, and that mandate was to continue the policies of Ronald Reagan. His failure to recognize this caused his defeat four years later.

It wasn't until June 1993 that Barbara Ehrenreich, writing the commentary "Essay" in *Time*, admitted that Clinton "was elected by a mere 43% of the voting public, hardly a mandate for sweeping change in any direction."

Actually, the idea of a Clinton landslide started well before the election. The 30 September *Washington Post* carried a story entitled, "Political Pundits Foresee a Landslide for Clinton." The subheading read, "Prediction Could Become Self-fulfilling." Indeed.

Chapter Eleven

Bush Whacking and Quayle Hunting through the Year

This chapter contains a miscellaneous list of further examples of media bias throughout the election year. However, just to show that the anti-Bush attitude of the media wasn't limited to 1992, we begin with one of many earlier examples.

The Split Screen Coincidence

On 21 December 1989, George Bush gave a press conference concerning the recent invasion of Panama. As onc would expect, he was upbeat about the success of the operation he had ordered. What he didn't know is that, at the precise same time, flag-draped coffins of the American servicemen lost in the invasion were being unloaded from a military planc. Threc different networks–NBC, ABC, and CNN–decided to present these two stories simultaneously, using a split screen. So, while Bush smiled and bantered lightly with reporters on one side of the screen, coffins were silently displayed on the other. The message that George Bush didn't care about the loss of life was unmistakable.

How often does one see two news stories presented side by side on split screen? Virtually all news stories are tape delayed, and the unloading of coffins is certainly not a story that would have suffered by being delayed for five minutes. The idea that all three of these networks hit on the idea of this seldom-used technique out of mere coincidence strains the imagination. Two more realistic possibilities are that two of the networks stole it from another or, worse, that each network was deliberately looking for ways to make Bush look bad.

The worst of it, of course, is that Bush did not know that his upbeat attitude was being juxtaposed against the bodies of dead Americans. The White House received hundreds of angry calls and letters. The president called another press conference at which he begged the media to help him set the record straight. "I could understand why the viewers were concerned about this. They thought their president at a solemn moment like that didn't give a damn. And I do. I do. I feel it so strongly. So please help me with that if you would." Happily, NBC, ABC, and CNN covered the controversy in some detail that evening. On CBS, Dan Rather reported only that Bush had criticized some television networks because "he did not like the showing of flag-draped coffins coming home at the same time his last news conference was going on."

The Party's Over

On the night of the New Hampshire primary in January, ABC's Jeff Greenfield reported from the headquarters of the Bush campaign. As they were wrapping things up around midnight, David Brinkley noticed on his monitor that the Bush victory party had ended. "Let's use it," said producer Jeff Gralnick. He told Greenfield to remain silent as they panned the room. As they did, Brinkley said several times, "Jeff, are you there?," suggesting that the Bush camp had gone home, discouraged.

The Los Angeles Riots

George Bush's reaction to the Los Angeles riots is an unfortunate example of his people-pleasing. His initial statement following the verdict was that the "system had worked," but when he saw the rage of the riots and the nationwide response, he quickly issued a second statement which directly contradicted the first. The verdict was a "travesty," he said, and he pledged that the federal government would step in and try the police officers for the violation of Rodney King's civil rights.

Politicians are supposed to play politics; the media is not. Bush addressed the nation two days after the riots, urging peace. In an unprecedented move, Peter Jennings decided to allow Bill Clinton a chance to respond to the presidential speech. Even ABC executive vice-president Richard Wald was upset by this. According to Tom Rosensteil in *Strange Bedfellows*, Wald summoned Jennings and producer Jeff Gralnick to his office:

> "This is wrong!" he yelled at Jennings. "This is a presidential occasion. A state of emergency, and the President has a right to go to the nation and speak to the people without making it a political occasion."
>
> "If Bush had given this speech last night I would agree with you," Jennings answered. "But Bush had already taken his action as president, calling out the troops, the night before. Tonight, he was just making a campaign speech."

In other words, news anchor Peter Jennings has the right to decide when and how a president should address the nation on a given issue, as well as the right to decide when a presidential address is legitimate or merely political. This was the same media that so often said they should just present the truth and let people decide for themselves.

Waiting for Perot

On 21 June, the *Washington Post* headline read, "Perot Investigated Bush's Activities." This was a two-for-one for the liberal newspaper because it made Perot and Bush both look bad. But, the story, written by Bob Woodward and John Mintx, concerned a 1987 effort by Perot to check the legitimacy of a large tax deduction taken by a friend of Bush, not Bush himself. Deep inside the story, on an inside page, was the strange comment that Perot had passed the information he had gathered on to the *Post* on the condition that he would not be named as the source.

The story caused Perot to hold a press conference in which he confirmed the story and said that the *Post* had gone on to investigate the story itself. This would then make the paper guilty of the very thing of which it was accusing Perot. This, in turn, led the *Post* to assign reporter Howard Kurtz to, basically, investigate itself. Kurtz found that Bob Woodward, one of the authors of the new story, had been the reporter who had received Perot's information four years before. Kurtz also quoted Perot's press secretary James Squires as saying, "It was Woodward who was investigating Bush." Woodward confirmed that he had been doing a series of investigative reports on Bush, suggesting that Perot had heard about these reports and had given his information to Woodward to help with that effort.

All of which means that the *Post*'s story about Perot investigating Bush was at the very least hypocritical, since the *Post* was doing precisely the same thing. Also, at the very least, the *Post* revealed the name of an anonymous source–Perot, in this case–

contradicting a right it so vehemently claims for itself when called on to justify its actions.

The *Times*: 0 for 2

On 16 August, the morning before the Republican National Convention opened, the *New York Times* ran a story suggesting that President Bush's health wasn't good enough to handle the strain of campaigning. This did not turn out to be true, of course.

Worse, a second story reported that Bush might attack Iraq for political purposes, stating that the information came from an "unnamed" senior official within the administration. The head of the U.N. inspection team in Iraq strongly denied that they were pushing or provoking Iraq in order to force a showdown. On "CBS This Morning" the next day, correspondent David Martin reported that he had just spoken to a senior Pentagon official who didn't even know where the inspection team was or what they were doing. "This notion," says Martin, "that there was this set-up job in which the U.S. was telling the U.N. inspectors exactly where to go and that it would be a provocative spot that would immediately trigger an air strike just isn't standing up under the light of scrutiny." The *Times* never disavowed or corrected either story.

"Will You Shut Up?"

Bush was heckled at the conference of the League of Families by family members who thought their prisoner-of-war relatives might still be alive in Vietnam. Network cameras caught these people chanting, showing them to be average wives and mothers. The cameras then showed President Bush angrily saying, "Will you sit down and shut up?" Trouble is, the person Bush told to "sit down and shut up" was not a family member, but an unknown person who started rambling about blacks and the homeless and would not stop. After Bush's rebuke, this person left the room immediately, suggesting that he had no real business there. Nevertheless, Bush's outburst got wide attention.

A month later, Bill Clinton was giving a speech in Chicago when a heckler began ranting about adultery. Clinton angrily told the protestor to "sit down and shut up." This outburst drew almost no media attention.

In Little Rock in September, when Bill Clinton was accosted when leaving church by three hundred protestors complaining about his stance on issues such as gay rights, not a single story showed up in the national media or on the network news shows. The Associated Press distributed a photograph but no story. The *Los Angeles Times* even mentioned that he had gone to church but said nothing about the protest.

Wherever He Goes Is Wrong

John Dancy, on the "NBC Nightly News" on 29 August, said, "There's a huge pool of economic anger in these small towns, and Clinton is trying to exploit it. . . . In the heart of America, Clinton is finding the hurt of America."

But, in the very next story, correspondent Tom Pettit had this to say about Dan Quayle doing precisely what Clinton was doing: "Quayle also likes working obscure small towns in the South. . . . The Quayle campaign stop begins to resemble Disney World's Main Street—the crowds predominantly white. . . . Why is Quayle avoiding big cities?" Because, says Michael Beschloss, "The strategy is to keep him away from places he can do harm." Pettit continues, "Right now, he is presenting his vision to the America of the past—small town America."

Great Expectations

Throughout the year, the media justified negative reporting on Bush on the grounds that he had failed to live up to expectations that the media itself had set. Bush did not have to lose a primary or a debate, he had simply to do *less well* than the media said he needed to do. So, even when Bush was winning, he could be made into a loser.

Pat Buchanan showed a surprising strength in the polls leading up to the New Hampshire primary. The pundits and commentators eventually decided that George Bush was in serious trouble if Pat Buchanan could secure 40 percent or more of the vote. When exit polls suggested that he had, the television reports that night and the newspaper reports the next morning portrayed Bush as a loser. When the votes were counted, it turned out that Buchanan had secured only 33 percent of the votes. It was later discovered that there was an error in the polling questions.

The same thing held true at the Republican National Convention. Pundits and reporters spoke of Bush's need to "hit a homerun" and to "give the best speech of his political career." Their reaction to his speech, which was certainly a good one, was barely disguised scorn, not because there was anything wrong with it, but because it hadn't performed the necessary miracle.

The scenario was repeated with the presidential debates. Bush didn't do anything wrong, but he failed to hit the "homerun" the media said he needed. Commentators on every network harped on this. An Associated Press wire that night said, "Debate Coaches Agree: Bush Lost." John Dancy said on NBC's "Today" show the next morning, "Clinton did what he had to do and Bush did not." The *Boston Herald* tabloid's headline was "Bush Strikes Out." By the next night,

NBC's John Cochran was reporting that "the Bush people are getting very, very tired of hearing that the President didn't hit a homerun last night."

Kickoff Coverage

Accuracy in Media analyzed the coverage on Labor Day—traditionally the opening day of the general campaign—by the "CBS Evening News." Each candidate received about two minutes of coverage. In the four minutes, AIM counted nine negative items or statements about Bush and only two about Clinton, and one of those was a statement by Bush himself. Clinton received five positive statements while Bush got only three.

Accuracy in Media also analyzed the commentary in the *New York Times* in the month of September. Of nineteen columns written by staff members on the campaign, all were pro-Clinton or anti-Bush except for one column by William Safire criticizing the Clinton campaign for its poor organization of a rally. Of seventeen columns written by others—including syndicated columnists—fourteen were pro-Clinton or anti-Bush. In total, *Times* commentary ran ten-to-one in favor of Bill Clinton.

Pothead Quayle?

It was one of those rumors which, like the death of Paul McCartney, refused to go away. There was, supposedly, a man in prison who had tried to let the media know that he had once sold marijuana to Dan Quayle. As a result of these attempts, this man was denied parole, placed in solitary confinement, or both, depending on which version of the story you heard.

The rumor actually began during the 1988 campaign when Brett Kimberlin, a man serving a fifty-one-year term for drug smuggling, claimed to have sold marijuana to Quayle in the 1970s when he was a law student at Indiana University. Kimberlin could offer no proof that he had ever even met Quayle.

In 1990, another inmate contacted Don Hewitt, executive producer of "60 Minutes." Hewitt dispatched Morley Safer, who asked the accuser to submit to a lie detector test. The inmate twice failed the test, then broke down and cried in front of Safer. "I made it up," he said, "trying to get out of jail."

On 13 November 1991, the *Indianapolis Star*, having examined the Drug Enforcement Administration's file on Quayle, reported on a man named Charles Parker. Parker, arrested for selling drugs, told agents that one of his customers had bragged about selling cocaine to Quayle. This customer, Terry Carson, was questioned by agents. He testified that he had made the story up to impress Parker, and he passed a lie detector test confirming that.

The idea of Dan Quayle smoking pot is, of course, almost as humorous as an image of George Bush running around having lascivious affairs. Nevertheless, although journalists had investigated the story and found it to be pure fabrication, the rumor somehow managed to surface sporadically throughout the 1992 campaign. For example, the October issue of the *New Yorker* contained a long piece by Mark Singer, a shortened version of which appeared on the op-ed page of the *New York Times* on 16 October. This piece implicitly accused the 1988 Bush campaign of asking the Justice Department to place Brett Kimberlin in solitary confinement.

Gary Trudeau, in his comic strip "Doonesbury," ran a long series suggesting the story was true. Not a single paper refused to run the false accusations made by the strip, nor did any run a notice pointing it out. It is easy to dismiss this on the grounds that it is, after all, only a comic strip. But, "Doonesbury" presents itself as reality-based and prides itself on social satire. In many papers, it runs on the editorial page. Trudeau's lampooning gave the appearance of a serious satire on a real coverup. Even this could be easily dismissed if the rumors had not been proven false by the very papers that ran the "Doonesbury" strips.

The Not-So-Great Debates

Prior to the vice-presidential debate, NBC reporter Andrea Mitchell warned, "Look out for Stockdale. I think he's going to be very engaging." *Newsweek* reporter Clara Bingham said, "I think it's going to be especially difficult for Quayle, because he's got two really smart people he's debating against. . . . He's got another unknown in Stockdale, who's really going to be hard for him to hold a candle to intellectually."

During the second presidential debate, held at the University of Richmond, a young black woman asked the candidates to explain how they had personally been affected by the national debt. "How has the national debt personally affected each of your lives? And if it hasn't, how can you honestly find a cure for the economic problems of the common people if you have no experience in what's ailing them?"

The question was obviously aimed at George Bush because he was the only one of the three who had never experienced economic hardship. Bush, recognizing this, hesitated.

> **Bush:** If the question–maybe I–get it wrong. Are you suggesting that if somebody has means that the national debt doesn't affect them?
>
> **Audience Member:** What I'm saying is. . . .
>
> **Bush:** I'm not sure I get it. Help me with the question and I'll try to answer it.
>
> **Audience Member:** Well, I've had friends who have been laid off from jobs. I know people

> who cannot afford to pay the mortgage on their homes, their car payment. . . .

Finally, moderator Carole Simpson stepped in to point out that the questioner was actually referring to the recession, not the national debt. Once this point was made, Bush went on to answer adequately. But, it was too late. His phrase "I'm not sure I get it" was seized on by both the Clinton campaign and the media to illustrate a point favorable to the Democrats–George Bush just "didn't get it" when it came to the economic problems of America.

Had Bush been thinking clearly, he might have pointed out that Bill Clinton–whose salary had been paid by taxpayers most of his adult life and whose wife was wealthy in her own right–could hardly claim to be impacted by the recession in any significant way.

Debatable Tactics

Carole Simpson of ABC News, who moderated this debate and who set feminism back a decade or so by treating the presidential candidates like little children, claimed that there had been no prescreening of the audience questions. But, Rush Limbaugh found sources claiming that Simpson had indeed spent time prior to the broadcast talking with audience members, and one of the things she asked was what questions they would ask if called on.

A Reporter Tells the Truth

Following the vice-presidential debate, Bush-Quayle press secretary Torie Clarke was approached by a national network news reporter. He told her he thought Quayle had done a good job and won the debate. "Why didn't you say that in your story?" she asked. "If I had said that on the air," he said, "my network would have killed me."

Non-Revelations

Also in October, the press publicized comments by Gen. Richard Secord concerning Iran-Contra as "new revelations," when, in reality, these comments were merely Secord's opinion and contained no new evidence. The comments of former national security aide Howard Teicher were dramatized as if they contradicted what Bush had said, but they didn't.

The Floyd Brown of Democrats?

Ever heard of James Brosnahan? If you haven't, it can only be because the investigative powers of the press suspiciously failed once again.

James Brosnahan is a lawyer in the San Francisco office of special prosecutor Lawrence Walsh. Walsh, as you know, had been investigating the Iran-Contra affair since the middle of Reagan's second term. Although he had spent as much as $100 million of taxpayer money, he had failed to secure one major conviction, and he had made no secret of his frustration.

One of those Walsh had indicted had been Reagan's defense secretary, Casper Weinberger, but that case had been thrown out of court. On 30 October, just four days before the election, Walsh's office handed down a new indictment of Weinberger. Included in the indictment were new materials which implied that George Bush had known about the arrangement, knowledge Bush had repeatedly denied. One reporter, Deborah Orin of the *Washington Post*, was honest enough to call the indictment "suspiciously timed." Nevertheless, the press pursued the story aggressively in the final days of the campaign, placing Bush on the defensive and reversing the trend toward a narrowing gap between himself and Clinton.

It was James Brosnahan who handed down this suspiciously timed indictment. Who is Brosnahan? Well, in 1986, he had attempted to sabotage the elevation of conservative Supreme Court Justice William Rehnquist to the position of chief justice by charging him with racism, charges he refused to repeat under oath. In other words, Brosnahan is a highly partisan Democrat. He was also a contributor to the Clinton campaign.

After the election, the *Washington Times* reported that Brosnahan had leaked the new indictment to the Clinton campaign in advance, allowing the Democrats time to mobilize against the president. A press release prepared by the Clinton campaign was dated 29 October, the day before the indictment was filed. Such a leak, if it did occur, would be a violation of legal ethics. Yet, the press accepted George Stephanopoulos's explanation that the date of the release was a "typo" and dropped the story.

In short, there is very good reason to believe that Brosnahan used his government, taxpayer-funded position to sabotage a presidential election, which is itself a clear violation of federal law. Despite this, neither the press nor the government undertook to investigate Brosnahan's actions, and there is little question that his "October surprise" had a very real effect on the outcome of the election.

Stephanopoulos the Speed-Dialer

How did the Clinton campaign use the information? It couldn't have done much without the help of the media, but that wasn't far behind. The Friday night before the election, President Bush appeared on a special edition of "Larry King Live." King opened with the subject of the Iran-Contra affair. King then went to the phones and feigned surprise when Clinton press secretary George Stephanopoulos quickly made it through the mass of callers. Bush himself implied that Stephanopoulos had gotten favored treatment, but King insisted that this was not the case.

"This is an open phones session," King said. "He dialed in directly. It wasn't a secret number." After Stephanopoulos had finished grilling the president, Bush sighed, "It's wonderful how this call gets in, this random call. . . ." "We don't have a private line," King insisted. "We really don't. I don't control the calls."

In reality, it was quickly learned, the show's producer had given Stephanopoulos a special telephone number so he could get through and grill the president. The producer said that King "misspoke" in saying that there was no private line and that Stephanopoulos had not been given a special number. When a caller the next day charged that Bush had been "set up," King virtually admitted he had lied by saying, "Mr. Stephanopoulos called. He had a complaint. We told him to call back." If you and I called Larry King prior to a show with a "complaint," do you think we'd be given a special number to "call back"?

Your Tax Dollars at Work

The Public Broadcasting System's election night coverage came from the studio of WGBH in Boston. The three-hour show, called "The Finish Line," was co-hosted by former Carter official Hodding Carter and liberal journalist Ken Walker. The analysts were liberal commentators Ellen Goodman, Anthony Lewis, and Daniel Schoor, along with liberal activist Roger Wilkins. PBS election coverage prior to election night had been handled by such luminous liberals as Bill Moyers—LBJ's former press agent—and William Greider. Election-year specials had been hosted by former Democratic congresswoman Barbara Jordan and Henry Cisneros, who would wind up on Clinton's cabinet.

When the election night line-up was announced, Republican Sen. Bob Dole charged that PBS's election coverage would be "tilted so far to the left, your TV may fall over." Almost immediately, the producer of the program announced that Senator Dole and other conservatives would be invited to participate. While this was heartening to those who believe in balanced coverage, the new invitations were clearly a hurried attempt to appease critics in Congress, which controls the PBS purse string.

Despite the addition of some conservative faces, the coverage on election night remained heavily tilted to the political left. Late in the evening, for example, when it was announced that Ohio's returns had put Clinton over the top, there were loud cheers and applause heard from off-camera. Even Richard Carlson, president of the Corporation for Public Broadcasting, said, "It was like handing a gift to our critics. The WGBH production that night was biased, unbalanced, unprofessional, and boring. The camera work was awful, and the cheering for Clinton was pronounced and sustained."

PBS officials always deny such charges of bias. Yet, that very summer, PBS had lobbied hard to defeat language in its funding legislation that would require objectivity in its programming. If PBS is unbiased, why would it fear such language?

Photo Opportunities

Toward the end of the campaign, readers wrote into the *Washington Post* asking if it was purposefully choosing bad photographs of the president. Finally, Joann Byrd of the *Post* conducted her own study of the photos used during the debates. Sure enough, Clinton's photos made him look good three times out of four, while Bush's made him look bad about half the time.

The Vanishing Crowds

At a postelection seminar sponsored by the Brookings Institute, Bush campaign press secretary

Torie Clarke reported a pattern of discrimination by reporters during the campaign. For example, while the press generally allowed Clinton the chance to respond to what Bush said, it did not allow Bush the same courtesy. In fact, it got to the point that some reporters even refused to accept Clarke's phone calls when she wanted to respond to something Clinton had said. In another case, a reporter for a national newspaper was consistently publishing smaller crowd estimates for Bush events than were other reporters. When Clarke confronted the reporter about this, her only response was a blunt, "Yeah, you're right."

Some Final (Rather Biased) Words

During the Republican National Convention, CBS anchorman Dan Rather was seen upbraiding one of the security personnel who was wearing a very popular lapel sticker bearing the CBS logo and the words "Rather Biased." Rather insisted that he made every effort to ensure the objectivity and fairness of his broadcasts.

But, in May 1993, Rather was speaking via satellite to President Clinton during a meeting of CBS affiliates when the president wished him luck in his new on-air partnership with Connie Chung. "If we could be one-hundredth as great as you and Hillary Rodham Clinton have been together in the White House," Rather replied, "we'd take it right now and walk away winners." He closed with, "God bless you. Tell Mrs. Clinton we respect her and we're pulling for her."

Chapter Twelve

Conclusion: We Need Another "New Covenant"

In the early days of our republic, a wide variety of highly partisan newspapers thundered their opinions in a cacophony of attacks and defenses. Every party and movement produced its own broadside and distributed it on the streets. Hot political debate among average citizens was the norm, and it was fueled by the splintered nature of the press.

Things have changed since then. A growing population and improved printing technology made it too expensive for small groups to publish and distribute to the general public. Radio and television became the vehicle for communicating dissenting views to the public, but the rise of the television network took customers away from radio, leading to a monopolization of views. Television also took customers from the newspapers, so that most cities were left with only one daily. Today, most people receive their news from the networks, two or three magazines, and their local paper.

None of which would be a problem were it not for the fact that this small cadre of information distributors tend overwhelmingly to be of one ideological mind. Studies have repeatedly shown that more than 80 percent of journalists vote Democratic. Journalists are much more likely to support such agendas as gay rights than is the average American. Yet, it is the nature of bias that most journalists are convinced that their views are "mainstream."

Still, liberal bias is only part of the problem. The other part of the problem was amply demonstrated once Clinton was in office. The very media that had helped to elect him turned on him with a vengeance. They had done the same to Jimmy Carter during his presidency.

The media uses this bipartisan bashing as its biggest defense. On 26 August, Bob Beckel and Sam Donaldson, sitting on the left on "Crossfire," did not deny that the media was hard on Bush. But, they insisted that they had been just as hard on Clinton by publicizing the allegations of draft dodging and marital infidelity. In a forum on C-SPAN just after the election, Mara Liasson, a reporter for National Public Radio, predicted that the media would give Clinton a hard time. This will show, she said, that rather than having a liberal bias, the media merely have a tendency to bash the powers that be.

Many of us might ask, why is it the job of the media to bash anyone at all? Why don't they just report the facts? Bashing authority is an agenda in itself, and one that is easily explained by the fact that those in power in today's media came of age in the turbulent sixties. This is hardly a defense for the media; it rather confirms an anti-authoritarian bias that necessarily must be antigovernment, antichurch, antibusiness, and antifamily. Thus, while this bias will tend to be hard on both parties, it will always be harder on conservatives.

Is this the type of news media we want? The massive changes in the news industry of the last thirty years have led us to a crossroads. The American people must decide whether they will continue supporting and listening to an untrustworthy media. Government (thank goodness) can do nothing to infringe on the freedom of the press, but Americans can let their frustration be known and demand a change.

In the past, this battle has been fought on ideological grounds, with conservatives attacking the media's liberal bias. But, it is not just conservatives who are unhappy with the media. Many civil rights leaders, for example, charge that the media perpetuates stereotypes by focusing on blacks who are inner-city poor, criminals, or drug users. Many women feel betrayed by the media's allegiance to the radical brand of feminism.

The time has come to take the battle to a new level–that of consumer advocacy. In a very real sense, the news is a consumer product–through subscription fees and subscribers, we pay these organizations to find out what is going on and report it to us. When this information is incomplete, slanted, or distorted, we, as consumers, are receiving a flawed product. And, as consumers, we should have recourse. If media monitoring groups and average citizens band together to make their displeasure known–and to impose boycotts if necessary–the media and their corporate owners would be forced to pay attention.

Ideally, of course, consumers would work in cooperation with the media to increase objectivity and restore balance. Part of the effort must include the education of journalists concerning those groups and ideas which they have stereotyped as intolerant. Concrete goals such as strengthening the nebulous ethical standards of the industry should be set. Overall, consumers must make it clear that they are sick and tired of advocacy journalism.

When Bill Clinton misappropriated Scripture to declare a "New Covenant" between America's government and her people, the media cheered. The ostensible reason for the need for a new covenant is that the government has failed to fulfill its purpose in a changing world. If so, an argument can be made for the need for a new covenant between America's news industry and the people it serves, for surely today's media is failing to properly inform the public. Since the media seems to support the idea of a revised task for government and a new relationship between government and the people, should they not be equally willing to revise their own methods and purpose?

Appendix A

Complete Transcripts of the Gennifer Flowers/Bill Clinton Tapes

Reprinted from a press release distributed by Gennifer Flowers at her press conference of 28 January 1992.

Flowers: Are you there? Sorry about that. Mother was . . . wanted me to get her a glass of water. See that was another thing. See, my parents are here, and I'll tell you what, the last thing I needed was to . . .

Clinton: Have that happen . . .

Flowers: . . . have that happen cause my mother would get very concerned and worried and so far you know . . .

Clinton: [garbled] If they ever hit you with it just say "no" and go on, there's nothing they can do.

Flowers: Well I will, but I mean . . . I . . . you know . . . she's my mother and you know how mothers can be.

Clinton: They don't want to hear it at all.

Flowers: Well, she would just get all in a tizzy about . . . about it and uh, so I thought "Good God, that's all I need." Cause they're, uh, they're gonna be here . . . well they're leaving Wednesday morning and they were at the club tonight and they'll be here tomorrow night, which, you know, parents do. And I thought, "Oh, please Jesus, don't let those people be out there."

Clinton: I'm just sorry that you ever had to put up with that [next word is garbled].

Flowers: Well, you know, to be real honest with you, I'm not completely surprised. I didn't think it would start this quickly. But I think, Bill, you're being naive if you think that these other shows like "Current Affair" and, oh, what are some of the others, uh . . .

Clinton: Well, I thought they . . .

Flowers: "Hard Copy."

Clinton: I thought they'd look into it. But, you know, I just think a crazy person like Larry Nichols is not enough to get a story on the television with names in it.

Flowers: Right. Well, he better not get on there and start naming names.

Clinton: Well, that's what I mean. You know, if all the people who are named . . . deny it . . . That's all, I mean, I expect them to come look into it and interview you and everything, uh, but I just think that if everybody's on record denying it you've got no problem.

Flowers: Well, I don't think . . . I don't think it . . . I don't . . . Well, why would they waste their money and time coming down here unless someone showed 'em some interest? See, they weren't here tonight and they're not going to be there.

Clinton: No, no. See, that's it. I mean, they're gonna run this Larry Nichols thing down, they're gonna try to goad people up, you know, but if everybody kinda hangs tough, they're just not going to do anything. They can't.

Flowers: No. They can't.

Clinton: They can't run a story like this unless somebody said, "Yeah, I did it with him."

[end of first segment]

Clinton: I'll tell you what, it would be extremely valuable if they ever do run anybody by me, you know. If they ever get anybody to do this, just to have, like I told you before when I called you, is to have an on-file affidavit explaining that, you know, you were approached by a Republican and asked to do that.

Flowers: Mm hmm. Well . . .

Clinton: [garbled] . . . the more I think about it, you should call him back . . . [garbled] . . . just don't know.

Flowers: Well, I think that . . . Well, are you going to run? [laughs] Can you tell me that?

Clinton: I want to. I wonder if I'm going to be blown out of the water with this. I don't see how they can [garbled word] so far.

Flowers: I don't think they can. . . .

Clinton: If they don't, if they don't have pictures . . .

Flowers: Mh hmm.

Clinton: . . . which they [garbled] . . . anybody and no one says anything then they don't have anything and arguably if someone says something, they don't have much.

Flowers: If they could blow you out of the water they would have already blown you. I really believe that because I believe that there are various ones that have been trying hard lately. See, like that "Inside Edition." Uh, there've probably been other sources too. [Pause] So . . . I don't think so. I honestly don't. That's my gut feeling. I would tell you if I did. [pause] But . . . you may know more about . . .

Clinton: How do you like holding [garbled word] . . . future in . . . [garbled word] hands? . . . Do you like that?

Flowers: Yeah. [laughs] No. Well, if it's positive I do, you know. I mean cause I want you to . . . I would love to see you go . . . Oh, I'd love to see you be President. I think that would be wonderful. I think you'd make a, a damn good one. I don't like Bush. I think he's a sneaky bastard. [laughs] [garbled] He's two-faced. I'd just love to see somebody get in there for a change, really make a difference. But uh . . . It's like I told you before, whatever you need me to do, just let me know.

Clinton: I will.

[end of segment two]

Flowers: . . . remember a long time ago when you called me and said that if you announced for, well, it was back the first time you were going to announce for, uh . . .

Clinton: Governor?

Flowers: No. President [laughs] [garbled] And you said [garbled] "Gennifer, just wanted you to know that there might be some reporters or something out there" and you said, "Now, uh, you be sure to [garbled words] [both laugh] say 'there's nothing to the rumor,' " and I said, O.K., I, well I shouldn't even say this to you, probably embarrass you. Do you remember what I said to you?

Clinton: No. What'd you say?

Flowers: I said, "Well, at the time you eat good ——." [laughs]

Clinton: What?

Flowers. I said I had to tell them that you ate good —— and you said, "Well you can tell them that if I don't run for President" [laughs]. I've got to keep my voice down, my parents are in the other . . . [laughs] [garbled]

Clinton: [garbled]

Flowers: And I thought, you know that's not real funny right now. But anyway I try to find the humor in things.

Clinton: Don't I know it. [garbled] [garbled]

Flowers: Well, I can guarantee you that's not something I've thought about [laughs], that's not the first thing on my mind when I think about those reporters being down there.

Clinton: God.

Flowers: Oh, Lord.

Clinton: [garbled]

Flowers: But, anyway, I think we're O.K. for now.

Clinton: [garbled] . . . we have to watch as we go along.

Flowers: Well, you're uh, you know, from the feedback I'm getting around me about various things that are going on with what you're doing, I'm getting very positive feedback.

Clinton: Yeah, there's no negative except this.

Flowers: This is the only thing.

Clinton. And there's no negative to me running except this and even if I win . . . as a matter of fact it might be better for me to lose the primary, I might lose the nomination to Bob Kerrey because he's um . . . got all the Gary Hart/Hollywood money and because he's single, looks like a movie star, won the Medal of Honor, and since he's single, nobody cares if he's screwing. [laughs]

[end of segment three]

[Dial tone]

[Dialing sounds]

[Ringing]

Voice: Governor's mansion, Roger Creek.

Flowers: Is Bill Clinton in please?

Voice: M'am, he's with some people right now. May I ask who's calling?

Flowers: This is Gennifer Flowers, I'm returning his call.

Voice: Gennifer Fowler?

Flowers: Flowers.

Voice: O.K. Hang on just a second.

Flowers: All right.

[long pause]

Clinton: Hello?

Flowers: Bill?

Clinton: Hey.

Flowers: It's Gennifer.

Clinton: How ya doin?

Flowers: Well, I'm fine, it hardly sounds like you.

Clinton: Oh, I'm having terrible throat problems.

Flowers: [cough] You're making me want to clear my throat. Can you talk? Can you talk a second?

Clinton: Yes.

Flowers: Uh, I'm sorry I had missed your call. I went up to see my mother for a few days.

Clinton: That's what I figured. How's she doin?

Flowers: Well, she's, she's doing O.K. physically. . . .

[end of segment four]

Flowers: Hello?

Clinton: Gennifer?

Flowers: Yes.

Clinton: It's Bill Clinton.

Flowers: Hi Bill.

Clinton: Hey I tried to call ya. I can't believe I got ya.

Flowers: Well whendya try to call me?

Clinton: Last night. Late.

Flowers: Well I was here.

Clinton: Did you take your phone off the hook?

Flowers: Well, I did, I . . . Well, I've been getting these hang-up calls . . . .

Clinton: Oh.

Flowers: . . . and at one point I took my phone . . . I, well, I didn't take it off the hook, I just, uh . . .

Clinton: Turned it off?

Flowers: Yeah.

Clinton: Oh that's what it was. I called . . . I started calling soon as I got home last night and I called for a couple of hours.

Flowers: Well, sorry I missed you.

Clinton: [garbled] . . . I was afraid I screwed up the number or something, and I kept calling.

Flowers: Well are you . . . you got a cold?

Clinton: Yeah. Oh it's just my . . . every year about this time I . . . My sinuses go bananas.

Flowers: Yeah, me too.

Clinton: And I've been in this stupid airplane too much, but I'm O.K.

Flowers: Well, good. Good. The reason I was calling was to tell you that, uh, well, a couple things. Uh, this last Wednesday, someone got into my apartment.

Clinton: Hold on a minute.

Flowers: O.K.

[long pause]

Clinton: O.K., I got it.

Flowers: Are you in Little Rock?

Clinton: No. . . .

Flowers: No.

Clinton: I am going to be there tonight late. I'm in, uh, Washington now and . . .

Flowers: Well . . .

Clinton: I'm going to Dallas, and then I'm coming to Little Rock.

Flowers: Uh, well . . .

Clinton: So somebody broke in your apartment?

Flowers: Well, yeah, well . . . There wasn't any sign of a break-in, uh, but the drawers and things . . . There wasn't anything missing that I can tell but somebody had . . .

Clinton: Somebody had gone through all your stuff?

Flowers: . . . And gone through my stuff.

Clinton: You think they were . . . But they didn't steal anything?

Flowers: No. No, my jewelry . . . I had jewelry here and everything, it was still here.

Clinton: You think they were trying to look for something on us?

Flowers: I think so. Well, I mean . . . why, why else? Um . . .

Clinton: You weren't missing any, any kind of papers or anything?

Flowers: Well, like what kind of papers?

Clinton: Well I mean did . . . any kind of personal records or checkbooks or anything like that? . . . Phone records?

Flowers: Do I have any?

Clinton: Yeah.

Flowers: Unh unh. I mean, why would I?

Clinton: I don't know I just . . .

Flowers: You . . . you usually call me, for that matter. And besides, who would know?

Clinton: Isn't that amazing?

Flowers: Even if I had it on my phone record . . . Oh, well, I guess they might be able to say "Oh well, you were in Washington on this date and maybe at that number and connect that but . . ."

Clinton: Well . . .

Flowers: See, you've always called me. So that's not a . . .

Clinton: I wouldn't care if they . . . you know, I, I . . . They may have my phone records on this computer here, but I don't think it . . . That doesn't prove anything.

Flowers: Well, that . . . that's true. But I just want to tell you about that.

Clinton: Wow.

Flowers: Let me tell you something positive.

Clinton: What?

Flowers: Uh, I heard, uh . . . I've heard a couple of people say . . . one had been to San Antonio, the other had been to Los Angeles. . . . and they both said that they were, uh, that all they heard out there was 'Clinton, Clinton, Clinton,' so . . .

Clinton: Really?

Flowers: Yeah. So I thought that was exciting.

Clinton: We've worked so hard.

Flowers: I know you have, but I . . . That may not be a lot, but I mean, that's a . . . I think that's a good indication.

Clinton: Well, no . . . Most people think, you know, that, except for Cuomo, I'm doing the best right now and uh . . . We're leading in the polls in Florida; . . . without Cuomo in there, but Cuomo's at 87 percent name recognition, and I have 54 percent so . . . I mean . . . I'm at a terrible disadvantage in name recognition still, but we're coming up, and . . . so I . . . We're moving pretty well, I'm really pleased about it.

Flowers: Well, I don't particularly care for Cuomo's uh, demeanor.

Clinton: Boy, he is so aggressive.

Flowers: Well, he seems like he could get real mean [laughs]

Clinton: [garbled]

Flowers: Yeah. . . . I wouldn't be surprised if he didn't have some mafioso major connections.

Clinton: Well he acts like one [laughs]

Flowers: Yeah.

[end of segment five]

Flowers: The only thing that concerns me, where I'm, I'm concerned at this point is the state job.

Clinton: Yeah, I never thought about that, but as long as you say you've just been looking for one, you'da check on it. If they ever ask you if you've talked to me about it, you can say no.

[end of segment six]

Flowers: Alright, darling, well you hang in there. I don't mean to worry you. I just . . .

Clinton: [garbled] . . . I just want to know these things and. . . . if I can help you, you let me know [garbled]

Flowers: Well, when you can help me is if I decide I want to get the heck out of here.

Clinton: All you need to do is let me know. . . .

Flowers: Because I don't know . . . I don't know where to turn. I really don't. I mean my contacts have just sort of fizzled in Nashville, it's been a long time and, I don't know, I don't know anybody.

Clinton: [garbled words] . . . I'll help you.

Flowers: O.K. Well, I'll, I'll be back in touch, and, uh, you will let me know if you know anything I need to know about.

Clinton: I will.

Flowers: O.K.? [laugh]

Clinton: Goodbye, baby.

Flowers: Talk to you later. Bye.

End of Transcripts—Gennifer Flowers-Bill Clinton

Appendix B

Bill Clinton's 3 December 1969 Letter to Lt. Col. Eugene Holmes, Director of the University of Arkansas ROTC Program

I am sorry to be so long in writing. I know I promised to let you hear from me at least once a month, and from now on you will, but I have had to have some time to think about this first letter. Almost daily since my return to England I have thought about writing, about what I want to and ought to say.

First, I want to thank you, not just for saving me from the draft, but for being so kind and decent to me last summer, when I was as low as I have ever been. One thing which made the bond we struck in good faith somewhat palatable to me was my high regard for you personally. In retrospect, it seems that the admiration might not have been mutual had you known a little more about me, about my political beliefs and activities. At least you might have thought me more fit for the draft than for ROTC.

Let me try to explain. As you know, I worked for two years in a very minor position on the Senate Foreign Relations Committee. I did it for the experience and the salary but also for the opportunity, however small, of working every day against a war I opposed and despised with a depth of feeling I had reserved solely for racism in America before Vietnam. I did not take the matter lightly but studied it carefully, and there was a time when not many people had more information about Vietnam at hand than I did.

I have written and spoken and marched against the war. One of the national organizers of the Vietnam Moratorium is a close friend of mine. After I left Arkansas last summer, I went to Washington to work in the national headquarters of the Moratorium, then to England to organize the Americans for the demonstrations Oct. 15 and Nov. 16.

Interlocked with the war is the draft issue, which I did not begin to consider separately until early 1968. For a law seminar at Georgetown I wrote a paper on the legal arguments for and against allowing, within the Selective Service System, the classification of selective conscientious objection, for those opposed to participation in a particular war, not simply to "participation in war in any form."

From my work I came to believe that the draft system itself is illegitimate. No government really rooted in limited, parliamentary democracy should have the power to make its citizens fight and kill and die in a war they may oppose, a war which even possibly may be wrong, a war which, in any case, does not involve immediately the peace and freedom of the nation.

The draft was justified in World War II because the life of the people collectively was at stake. Individuals had to fight, if the nation was to survive, for the lives of their countrymen and their way of life. Vietnam is no such case. Nor was Korea an example where, in my opinion, certain military action was justified but the draft was not, for the reasons stated above.

Because of my opposition to the draft and the war, I am in great sympathy with those who are not willing to fight, kill, and maybe die for their country (i.e. the particular policy of a particular government) right or wrong. Two of my friends at Oxford are conscientious objectors. I wrote a letter of recommendation for one of them to his Mississippi draft board, a letter which I am more proud of than anything else I wrote at Oxford last year. One of my roommates is a draft resister who is possibly under indictment and may never be able to go home again. He is one of the bravest, best men I know. That he is considered a criminal is an obscenity.

The decision not to be a resister and the related subsequent decisions were the most difficult of my life. I decided to accept the draft in spite of my beliefs for one reason: to maintain my political viability within the system. For years I have worked to prepare myself for a political life characterized by both practical political ability and concern for rapid social progress. It is a life I still feel compelled to try to lead. I do not think our system of government is by definition corrupt, however dangerous and inadequate it has been in recent years. (The society may be corrupt, but that is not the same thing, and if that is true we are all finished anyway.)

When the draft came, despite political convictions, I was having a hard time facing the prospect of fighting a war I had been fighting against, and that is why I contacted you. ROTC was the one way left in which I could possibly, but not positively, avoid both Vietnam and resistance. Going on with my education, even coming back to England, played no part in my decision to join ROTC. I am back here, and would have been at Arkansas Law School because there is nothing else I can do. In fact, I would like to have been able to take a year out perhaps to teach in a small college or work on some community action project and in the process to decide whether to attend law school or graduate school and how to begin putting what I have learned to use.

But the particulars of my personal life are not nearly as important to me as the principles involved. After I signed the ROTC letter of intent I began to wonder whether the compromise I had made with myself was not more objectionable than the draft would have been, because I had no interest in the ROTC program in itself and all I seemed to have done was to protect myself from physical harm. Also, I began to think I had deceived you, not by lies because there were none but by failing to tell you all the things I'm writing now. I doubt that I had the mental coherence to articulate them then.

At that time, after we had made our agreement and you had sent my 1-D deferment to my draft board, the anguish and loss of my self-regard and self confidence really set in. I hardly slept for weeks and kept going by eating compulsively and reading until exhaustion brought sleep. Finally, on Sept. 12 I stayed up all night writing a letter to the chairman of my draft board, saying basically what is in the preceding paragraph, thanking him for trying to help in a case where he really couldn't and stating that I couldn't do the ROTC after all and would he please draft me as soon as possible.

I never mailed the letter, but I did carry it on me every day until I got on the plane to return to England. I didn't mail the letter because I didn't see, in the end, how my going in the army and maybe going to Vietnam would achieve anything except a feeling that I had punished myself and gotten what I deserved. So I came back to England to try to make something of this second year of my Rhodes scholarship.

And that is where I am now, writing to you because you have been good to me and have a right to know what I think and feel. I am writing too in the hope that my telling this one story will help you to understand more clearly how so many fine people have come to find themselves still loving their country but loathing the military, to which you and other good men have devoted years, lifetimes, of the best service you could give. To many of us, it is no longer clear what is service and what is disservice, or if it is clear, the conclusion is likely to be illegal.

Forgive the length of this letter. There was much to say. There is still a lot to be said, but it can wait. Please say hello to Col. Jones for me.

Merry Christmas.

Sincerely,
Bill Clinton

Appendix C:

Vice-President Dan Quayle's Remarks to the Commonwealth Club of San Francisco, 19 May 1992

As you may know, I've just returned from a week-long trip to Japan. I was there to commemorate the 20th anniversary of the reversion of Okinawa to Japan by the United States, an act that has made a lasting impression on the Japanese.

While I was there, Japan announced its commitment to join with the United States in assisting Eastern and Central Europe with a 400 million dollar aid package. We also announced a manufacturing technology initiative that will allow American engineers to gain experience working in Japanese businesses.

Japan and the United States are allies and partners. Though we have our differences, especially in the area of trade, our two countries—with 40 percent of the world's GNP—are committed to a global partnership on behalf of peace and economic growth.

But in the midst of all of these discussions of international affairs, I was asked many times in Japan about the recent events in Los Angeles. From the perspective of many Japanese, the ethnic diversity of our culture is a weakness compared to their homogenous society. I begged to differ with my hosts. I explained that our diversity is our strength.

And I explained that the immigrants who come to our shores have made, and continue to make, vast contributions to our culture and our economy.

It is wrong to imply that the Los Angeles riots were an inevitable outcome of our diversified society. But the question that I tried to answer in Japan is one that needs answering here: What happened? Why? And how do we prevent it in the future?

One response has been predictable: Instead of denouncing wrongdoing, some have shown tolerance for rioters; some have enjoyed saying, "I told you so"; and some have simply made excuses for what happened. All of this has been accompanied by pleas for more money.

I'll readily accept that we need to understand what happened. But I reject the idea we should tolerate or excuse it.

When I have been asked during these last weeks who caused the riots and killing in L.A., my answer has been direct and simple: Who is to blame for the riots? The rioters are to blame. Who is to blame for the killing? The killers are to blame. Yes, I can understand how people were shocked and outraged by the verdict in the Rodney King trial. But there is simply no excuse for the mayhem that followed. To apologize or in any way to excuse what happened is wrong. It is a betrayal of all those people equally outraged and equally disadvantaged who did not loot and did not riot—and who were in many cases victims of the rioters. No matter how much you may disagree with the verdict, the riots were wrong. And if we as a society don't condemn what is wrong, how can we teach our children what is right?

But after condemning the riots, we do need to try to understand the underlying situation.

In a nutshell: I believe the lawless social anarchy which we saw is directly related to the breakdown of family structure, personal responsibility and social order in too many areas of our society. For the poor the situation is compounded by a welfare ethos that impedes individual efforts to move ahead in society, and hampers their ability to take advantage of the opportunities America offers.

If we don't succeed in addressing these fundamental problems, and in restoring basic values, any attempt to fix what's broken will fail. But one reason I believe we won't fail is that we have come so far in the last 25 years.

There is no question that this country has had a terrible problem with race and racism. The evil of slavery has left a long legacy. But we have faced racism squarely, and we have made progress in the past quarter century. The landmark civil rights bills of the 1960s removed legal barriers to allow full participation by blacks in the economic, social and political life of the nation. By any measure, the America of 1992 is more egalitarian, more integrated, and offers more opportunities to black Americans–and all minority group members–than the America of 1964. There is more to be done. But I think that all of us can be proud of our progress.

And let's be specific about one aspect of this progress: This country now has a black middle class that barely existed a quarter century ago. Since 1967 the median income of black two-parent families has risen by 60% in real terms. The number of black college graduates has skyrocketed. Black men and women have achieved real political power–black mayors head 48 of our largest cities, including Los Angeles. These are achievements.

But as we all know, there is another side to that bright landscape. During this period of progress, we have also developed a culture of poverty–some call it an underclass–that is far more violent and harder to escape than it was a generation ago.

The poor you will always have with you, Scripture tells us. And in America we have always had poor people. But in this dynamic, prosperous nation, poverty has traditionally been a stage through which people pass on their way to joining the great middle class. And if one generation didn't get very far up the ladder–their ambitious, better-educated children would.

But the underclass seems to be a new phenomenon. It is a group whose members are dependent on welfare for very long stretches, and whose men are often drawn into lives of crime. There is far too little upward mobility, because the underclass is disconnected from the rules of society. And these problems have, unfortunately, been particularly acute for black Americans.

Let me share with you a few statistics on the difference between black poverty in particular in the 1960s and now:

• In 1967, 68% of black families were headed by married couples. In 1991, only 48% of black families were headed by both a husband and wife.

• In 1965, the illegitimacy rate among black families was 28%. In 1989, 65%–two thirds–of all black children were born to never-married mothers.

• In 1951, 9.2% of black youth between 16 and 19 were unemployed. In 1965, it was 23%. In 1980, it was 35%. By 1989, the number had declined slightly, but was still 32%.

• The leading cause of death of young black males today is homicide.

It would be overly simplistic to blame this social breakdown on the programs of the Great Society alone. It would be absolutely wrong to blame it on the growth and success most Americans enjoyed during the 1980s. Rather, we are in large measure reaping the whirlwind of decades of changes in social mores.

I was born in 1947, so I'm considered one of those "Baby Boomers" we keep reading about. But let's look at one unfortunate legacy of the "Boomer" generation. When we were young, it was fashionable to declare war against traditional values. Indulgence and self-gratification seemed to have no consequences. Many of our generation glamorized casual sex and drug use, evaded responsibility and trashed authority. Today the "Boomers" are middle-aged and middle class. The responsibility of having families has helped many recover traditional values. And, of course, the great majority of those in the middle class survived the turbulent legacy of the 60s and 70s. But many of the poor, with less to fall back on, did not.

The intergenerational poverty that troubles us so much today is predominantly a poverty of values. Our inner cities are filled with children having children; with people who have not been able to take advantage of educational opportunities; with people who are dependent on drugs or the narcotic of welfare. To be sure, many people in the ghettos struggle very hard against these tides–and sometimes win. But too many feel they have no hope and nothing to lose. This poverty is, again, fundamentally a poverty of values.

Unless we change the basic rules of society in our inner cities, we cannot expect anything else to change. We will simply get more of what we saw three weeks ago. New thinking, new ideas, new strengths are needed.

For the government, transforming underclass culture means that our policies and programs must create a different incentive system. Our policies must be premised on, and must reinforce, values such as: family, hard work, integrity and personal responsibility.

I think we can all agree that government's first obligation is to maintain order. We are a nation of laws, not looting. It has become clear that the riots were fueled by the vicious gangs that terrorize the inner cities. We are committed to breaking those gangs and restoring law and order. As James Q. Wilson has written, "Programs of economic restructuring will not work so long as gangs control the streets."

Some people say "law and order" are code words. Well, they are code words. Code words for safety, getting control of the streets, and freedom from fear. And let's not forget that, in 1990, 84% of the crimes committed by blacks were committed against blacks.

We are for law and order. If a single mother raising her children in the ghetto has to worry about drive-by shootings, drug deals, or whether her children will join gangs and die violently, her difficult task becomes impossible. We're for law and order because we can't expect children to learn in dangerous schools. We're for law and order because if property isn't protected, who will build businesses?

As one step on behalf of law and order—and on behalf of opportunity as well—the President has initiated the "Weed and Seed" program—to "weed out" criminals and "seed" neighborhoods with programs that address root causes of crime. And we have encouraged community-based policing, which gets the police on the street so they can interact with citizens.

Safety is absolutely necessary. But it's not sufficient. Our urban strategy is to empower the poor by giving them control over their lives. To do that, our urban agenda includes:

• Fully funding the Home-ownership and Opportunity for People Everywhere program. HOPE, as we call it, will help public housing residents become home-owners. Subsidized housing all too often merely made rich investors richer. Home ownership will give the poor a stake in their neighborhoods, and a chance to build equity.

• Creating enterprise zones by slashing taxes in targeted areas, including zero capital gains tax, to spur entrepreneurship, economic development, and job creation in inner cities.

• Instituting our education strategy, AMERICA 2000, to raise academic standards and to give the poor the same choices about how and where to educate their children that rich people have.

• Promoting welfare reform to remove the penalties for marriage, create incentives for saving, and give communities greater control over how the programs are administered.

These programs are empowerment programs. They are based on the same principles as the Job Training Partnership Act, which aimed to help disadvantaged young people and dislocated workers to develop their skills to give them an opportunity to get ahead. Empowering the poor will strengthen families. And right now, the failure of our families is hurting America deeply. When families fail, society fails. The anarchy and lack of structure in our inner cities are testament to how quickly civilization falls apart when the family foundation cracks. Children need love and discipline. They need mothers and fathers. A welfare check is not a husband. The state is not a father. It is from parents that children learn how to behave in society; it is from parents above all that children come to understand values and themselves as men and women, mothers and fathers.

And for those concerned about children growing up in poverty, we should know this: marriage is probably the best anti-poverty program of all. Among families headed by married couples today, there is a poverty rate of 5.7%. But 33.4% of families headed by a single mother are in poverty today.

Nature abhors a vacuum. Where there are no mature, responsible men around to teach boys how to be good men, gangs serve in their place. In fact, gangs have become a surrogate family for much of a generation of inner-city boys.

I recently visited with some former gang members in Albuquerque, New Mexico. In a private meeting, they told me why they had joined gangs. These teenage boys said that gangs gave them a sense of security. They made them feel wanted, and useful. They got support from their friends. And, they said, "It was like having a family." "Like family." Unfortunately, that says it all.

The system perpetuates itself as these young men father children whom they have no intention of caring for, by women whose welfare checks support them. Teenage girls, mired in the same hopelessness, lack sufficient motive to say no to this trap.

Answers to our problems won't be easy.

We can start by dismantling a welfare system that encourages dependency and subsidizes broken families. We can attach conditions–such as school attendance, or work–to welfare. We can limit the time a recipient gets benefits. We can stop penalizing marriage for welfare mothers. We can enforce child support payments.

Ultimately, however, marriage is a moral issue that requires cultural consensus, and the use of social sanctions. Bearing babies irresponsibly is, simple, wrong. Failing to support children one has fathered is wrong. We must be unequivocal about this.

It doesn't help matters when prime time T.V. has Murphy Brown–a character who supposedly epitomizes today's intelligent, highly paid, professional woman–mocking the importance of fathers, by bearing a child alone, and calling it just another "lifestyle choice."

I know it's not fashionable to talk about moral values, but we need to do it. Even though our cultural leaders in Hollywood, network T.V., the national newspapers routinely jeer at them, I think that most of us in this room know that some things are good, and other things are wrong. Now it's time to make the discussion public.

It's time to talk again about family, hard work, integrity and personal responsibility. We cannot be embarrassed out of our belief that two parents, married to each other, are better in most cases for children than one. That honest work is better than handouts–or crime. That we are our brothers' keepers. That it's worth making an effort, even when the rewards aren't immediate.

So I think the time has come to renew our public commitment to our Judeo-Christian values—in our churches and synagogues, our civic organizations and our schools. We are, as our children recite each morning, "one nation under God." That's a useful framework for acknowledging a duty to an authority higher than our own pleasures and personal ambitions.

If we lived more thoroughly by these values, we would live in a better society. For the poor, renewing these values will give people the strength to help themselves by acquiring the tools to achieve self-sufficiency, a good education, job training, and property. Then they will move from permanent dependence to dignified independence.

Shelby Steele, in his great book, *The Content of Our Character*, writes, "Personal responsibility is the brick and mortar of power. The responsible person knows that the quality of his life is something that he will have to make inside the limits of his fate. . . . The quality of his life will pretty much reflect his efforts."

I believe that the Bush Administration's empowerment agenda will help the poor gain that power, by creating opportunity and letting people make the choices that free citizens must make.

Though our hearts have been pained by the events in Los Angeles, we should take this tragedy as an opportunity for self-examination and progress. So let the national debate roar on. I, for one, will join it. The president will lead it. The American people will participate in it. And as a result, we will become an even stronger nation.

Appendix D:

Pat Buchanan's Address to the Republican National Convention, 17 August 1992

Listen, my friends. We may have taken the long way home, but we finally got here to Houston. The first thing I want to do tonight is congratulate President George Bush and to remove any doubt about where we stand. The primaries are over, the heart is strong again, and the Buchanan Brigades are enlisted all the way to a great Republican comeback victory in November.

My friends, like many of you, last month I watched that giant masquerade ball up in Madison Square Garden, where 20,000 liberals and radicals dressed as moderates and centrists in the greatest single exhibition of cross-dressing in American political history.

You know, one by one, the prophets of doom appeared at the podium. The Reagan decade, they moaned, was a terrible time in America, and they said the only way to prevent worse times is to turn our country's fate and our country's future over to the party that gave us McGovern, Mondale, Carter, and Michael Dukakis. Where do they find these leaders?

No way, my friends. The American people are not going to go back to the discredited liberalism of the 1960s and the failed liberalism of the 1970s, no matter how slick the package in 1992.

The malcontents of Madison Square Garden notwithstanding, the 1980s were not terrible years in America; they were great years. You know it, and I know it, and everyone knows it except for the carping critics who sat on the sidelines of history, jeering at one of the greatest statesmen of modern times, Ronald Reagan.

Remember that time? Out of Jimmy Carter's "days of malaise," Ronald Reagan crafted the greatest peacetime economic recovery in history. Three million new businesses and 20 million new jobs. Under the Reagan Doctrine, one by one, it was the communist dominoes that began to fall. First, Grenada was liberated by U.S. airborne troops and the U.S. Marine Corps. Then the mighty Red Army was driven out of Afghanistan with American weapons. And then in Nicaragua, that squalid marxist regime was forced to hold free elections by Ronald Reagan's Contra army, and the communists were thrown out of power!

Fellow Americans, we ought to remember, it was under our party that the Berlin Wall came down and Europe was reunited. It was under our party that the Soviet empire collapsed and the captive nations broke free. You know, it is said, that every American president will be remembered in history with but a single sentence. George Washington was the father of his country. Abraham Lincoln freed the slaves and saved the Union. And Ronald Reagan won the cold war. And it is just about time that my old colleagues—the columnists and commentators looking down on us tonight from their sky boxes and anchor booths—gave Ronald Reagan the full credit he deserves for leading America to victory in the cold war.

Most of all, my friends, Ronald Reagan made us proud to be Americans again. We never felt better about our country and we never stood taller in the eyes of the world than when the Gipper was at the helm.

We're here tonight, my friends, not only to celebrate, but to nominate. An American president has many roles. He is our first diplomat. The architect of American foreign policy. And which of these two men is more qualified for that great role? George Bush has been U.N. Ambassador, director of the C.I.A., envoy to China. As vice-president, George Bush co-authored and co-signed the policies that won the cold war. As president, George Bush presided over the liberation of eastern Europe and the termination of the Warsaw Pact.

And what about Mr. Clinton? Well, Bill Clinton couldn't find 150 words to discuss foreign policy in an acceptance speech that lasted almost an hour. You know, as was said of another Democratic candidate, Bill Clinton's foreign policy experience is pretty much confined to having had breakfast at the International House of Pancakes.

Let's look at the record and recall what happened. Under President George Bush, more human beings escaped from the prison house of tyranny to freedom than in any other four-year period in history. And for any man to call this a record of failure is the cheap political rhetoric of politicians who only know how to build themselves up by tearing America down, and we don't want that kind of leadership in the United States.

The presidency, my friends, is also an office that Theodore Roosevelt called America's "bully pulpit." Harry Truman said it was preeminently a place of moral leadership. George Bush is a defender of right-to-life and a champion of the Judeo-Christian values and beliefs upon which America was founded.

Mr. Clinton, however, has a different agenda. At its top is unrestricted abortion on demand. When the Irish-Catholic governor of Pennsylvania asked to say a few words on behalf of the 25 million unborn children destroyed since *Roe v. Wade*, Bob Casey was told there was no room for him at the podium at Bill Clinton's convention, and no room at the inn. Yet a militant leader of the homosexual rights movement could rise at that same convention and say, "Bill Clinton and Al Gore represent the most pro-lesbian and pro-gay ticket in history," and so they do.

Bill Clinton says he supports school choice, but only for state-run schools. Parents who send their children to Christian schools or private schools or Jewish schools or Catholic schools need not apply.

Elect me, and you get two for the price of one, Mr. Clinton says of his lawyer spouse. And what does Hillary believe? Well, Hillary believes that 12-year-olds should have the right to sue their parents. And Hillary has compared marriage and the family as institutions to slavery and life on an Indian reservation. Well, speak for yourself, Hillary.

This, my friends, this is radical feminism. The agenda that Clinton and Clinton would impose on America: abortion on demand, a litmus test for the Supreme Court, homosexual rights, discrimination against religious schools, women in combat units. That's change, all right. But that's not the kind of change America needs. It's not the kind of change American wants. And it's not the kind of change we can abide in a nation we still call "God's country."

The president of the United States is also America's commander-in-chief. He's the man we authorize to send fathers and sons and brothers and friends into battle. George Bush was seventeen years old when they bombed Pearl Harbor. He left his high school graduation, he walked down to the recruiting office, and he signed up to become the youngest fighter pilot in the Pacific war.

And Mr. Clinton? And Bill Clinton? I'll tell you where he was. When Bill Clinton's time came in Vietnam, he sat up in a dormitory room at Oxford, England, and figured out how to dodge the draft. Let me ask the question to this convention: Which of these two men has won the moral authority to send young Americans into battle? I suggest respectfully it is the American patriot and war hero, Navy Lt. J.G. George Herbert Walker Bush.

My fellow Americans, this campaign is about philosophy. And it is about character. And George Bush wins hands down on both counts. And it's time all of us came home and stood beside him.

As his running mate, Mr. Clinton chose Al Gore. But just how moderate is Prince Albert? Well, according to the National Taxpayers Union, Al Gore beat out Teddy Kennedy two straight years for the title of biggest spender in the U.S. Senate, and Teddy Kennedy isn't moderate about anything. I'm not kidding about Teddy. How many other 60-year-olds do you know who still go to Florida for spring break?

You know, up at that great big costume party they held in New York, Mr. Gore made a startling declaration. "Henceforth," Albert Gore said, "the central organizing principle of governments everywhere must be the environment." Wrong, Albert. The central organizing principle of this republic is freedom. And from the ancient forests of Oregon and Washington to the inland empire of California, America's great middle class has got to start standing up to these environmental extremists who put ferns and rats and insects ahead of families and jobs.

One year ago, I could not have dreamt I would be here tonight. I was just one of many panelists on what President Bush calls "those crazy Sunday talk shows." But I disagreed with the President, and so we challenged the President in the primaries, and we fought as best we could. From February to June, President Bush won thirty-three of those primaries. I can't recall exactly how many we won; I'll get you the figure tomorrow. But tonight I do want to speak from the heart to the three million people who voted for Pat Buchanan for president. I will never forget you, or the honor you have done me. But I do believe, deep in my heart, that the right place for us to be now in this presidential campaign is right beside George Bush.

This party is my home, this party is our home, and we've gotta come home to it. And don't let anyone tell you different. Yes, we disagreed with President Bush, but we stand with him for the freedom to choose religious schools, and we stand with him against the amoral idea that gay and lesbian couples should have the same standing in law as married men and women. We stand with President Bush for the right-to-life and for voluntary prayer in the public schools. And we stand against putting our wives and daughters and sisters into the combat units of the United States Army. And we stand, my friends, we also stand with President Bush in favor of the right of small towns and communities to control the raw sewage of pornography that so terribly pollutes our popular culture. We stand with President Bush in favor of federal judges who interpret the law as written and against would-be Supreme Court justices like Mario Cuomo who think they have a mandate to rewrite the Constitution.

Friends, this election is about more than who gets what. It is about who we are. It is about what we believe and what we stand for as Americans. There is a religious war going on in this country. It is a cultural war as critical to the kind of nation we shall be as the cold war itself. But this war is for the soul of America. And in that struggle for the soul of

America, Clinton and Clinton are on the other side. George Bush is on our side.

[Buchanan reflects on his experiences on the campaign trail, giving several anecdotes and urging the Republican party to "reconnect" with those who are hurting economically. "They don't expect miracles of us, but they need to know we care." He speaks of a northwestern town that is "under the death penalty" due to a federal judge's decision to protect the habitat of the spotted owl. He also tells of those in Koreatown in Los Angeles who are bravely rebuilding following the recent riots.]

In these wonderful 25 weeks of our campaign, the saddest days were the days of that riot in L.A. The worst riot in American history. And out of that awful tragedy can come a message of hope. Hours after that riot ended, I went down to the Army compound in South Los Angeles, where I met the troopers of the 18th Cavalry, who had come to save the city of Los Angeles. An officer of the 18th Cav. said, "Mr. Buchanan, I want you to talk to a couple of our troopers." And I went over and I met these young fellows; they couldn't have been 20 years old. And they recounted their story.

They had come into Los Angeles late in the evening of the second day, and the rioting was still going on. And two of them walked up a dark street, where a mob had burned and looted every single building on the block but one—the convalescent home for the aged. And the mob was headed in to ransack and loot the apartments of the terrified old men and women inside. The troopers came up the street, M-16s at the ready, and the mob threatened and cursed, but the mob retreated, because it had met the one thing that could stop it: force rooted in justice and backed by moral courage. Greater love than this hath no man, than that he lay down his life for his friend. Here were 19-year-old boys, ready to lay down their lives to stop a mob from molesting old people they didn't even know.

And as those boys took back the streets of Los Angeles block by block, my friends, we must take back our cities, and take back our culture, and take back our country. God bless you, and God bless America.

More Good Books From Huntington House

Conservative, American & Jewish—
I Wouldn't Have It Any Other Way

by Jacob Neusner

Neusner has fought on the front lines of the culture war and here writes reports about sectors of the battles. He has taken a consistent, conservative position in the academy, federal agencies in the humanities and the arts, and in the world of religion in general and Judaism in particular. Engaging, persuasive, controversial in the best sense, these essays set out to change minds and end up touching the hearts and souls of their readers.

ISBN 1-56384-048-0 $9.99

Political Correctness:
The Cloning of the American Mind

by David Thibodaux, Ph.D.

The author, a professor of literature at the University of Southwestern Louisiana, confronts head on the movement that is now being called Political Correctness. Political correctness, says Thibodaux, "is an umbrella under which advocates of civil rights, gay and lesbian rights, feminism, and environmental causes have gathered." To incur the wrath of these groups, one only has to disagree with them on political, moral, or social issues. To express traditionally Western concepts in universities today can result in not only ostracism, but even suspension. (According to a recent "McNeil-Lehrer News Hour" report, one student was suspended for discussing the reality of the moral law with an avowed homosexual. He was reinstated only after he apologized.)

ISBN 1-56384-026-X Trade Paper $9.99

A Jewish Conservative Looks at Pagan America

by Don Feder

With eloquence and insight that rival contemporary commentators and essayists of antiquity, Don Feder's pen finds his targets in the enemies of God, family, and American tradition and morality. Deftly . . . delightfully . . . the master allegorist and Titian with a typewriter brings clarity to the most complex sociological issues and invokes giggles and wry smiles from both followers and foes. Feder is Jewish to the core, and he finds in his Judaism no inconsistency with an American Judeo-Christian ethic. Questions of morality plague school administrators, district court judges, senators, congressmen, parents, and employers; they are wrestling for answers in a "changing world." Feder challenges this generation and directs inquirers to the original books of wisdom: the Torah and the Bible.

ISBN 1-56384-036-7 Trade Paper $9.99
ISBN 1-56384-037-5 Hardcover $19.99

Don't Touch That Dial: The Impact of the Media on Children and the Family

by *Barbara Hattemer & Robert Showers*

Men and women without any stake in the outcome of the war between the pornographers and our families have come to the qualified, professional agreement that media does have an effect on our children—an effect that is devastatingly significant. Highly respected researchers, psychologists, and sociologists join the realm of pediatricians, district attorneys, parents, teachers, pastors, and community leaders—who have diligently remained true to the fight against filthy media—in their latest comprehensive critique of the modern media establishment (i.e., film, television, print, art, curriculum).

ISBN Quality Trade Paper 1-56384-032-4 $9.99
ISBN Hardcover 1-56384-035-9 $19.99

Gays & Guns
The Case against Homosexuals in the Military
by John Eidsmoe, Ph.D.

The homosexual revolution seeks to overthrow the Laws of Nature. A Lieutenant Colonel in the United States Air Force Reserve, Dr. John Eidsmoe eloquently contends that admitting gays into the military would weaken the combat effectiveness of our armed forces. This cataclysmic step would also legitimize homosexuality, a lifestyle that most Americans know is wrong.

While echoing Cicero's assertion that "a sense of what is right is common to all mankind," Eidsmoe rationally defends his belief. There are laws that govern the universe, he reminds us. Laws that compel the earth to rotate on its axis, laws that govern the economy; and so there is also a moral law that governs man's nature. The violation of this moral law is physically, emotionally and spiritually destructive. It is destructive to both the individual and to the community of which he is a member.

ISBN Trade Paper 1-56384-043-X $7.99
ISBN Hardcover 1-56384-046-4 $14.99

Homeless in America: The Solution
by Jeremy Reynalds

Author Jeremy Reynalds's current shelter, Joy Junction, located in Albuquerque, New Mexico, has become the state's largest homeless shelter. Beginning with fifty dollars in his pocket and a lot of compassion, Jeremy Reynalds now runs a shelter that has a yearly budget of over $600,000. He receives no government or United Way funding. Anyone who desires to help can, says Reynalds. If you feel a burden to help those less fortunate than you, read this book.

ISBN 1-56384-063-4 $9.99

I Shot an Elephant in My Pajamas— The Morrie Ryskind Story

by Morrie Ryskind with John H. M. Roberts

The Morrie Ryskind story is a classic American success story. The son of Russian Jewish immigrants, Ryskind went on to attend Columbia University and achieve legendary fame on Broadway and in Hollywood, win the Pulitzer Prize, and become a noted nationally syndicated columnist. Writing with his legendary theatrical collaborators George S. Kaufman and George and Ira Gershwin, their political satires had an enormous impact on the development of the musical comedy. In Hollywood, many classic films and four of the Marx Brothers' sublime romps also bear the signatory stamp of genius—Morrie Ryskind.

Forced by his increasingly conservative views to abandon script-writing in Hollywood, Ryskind had the satisfaction near the end of his life to welcome into his home his old friend, the newly elected President of the United States, Ronald Reagan.

ISBN 1-56384-000-6 $12.99

A Call to Manhood: In a Fatherless Society

by David E. Long

Western society is crumbling—from the collapse of the family...to our ailing economic system, from the scandals in the church...to the corruptions in the Halls of Congress, from the decline of business...to the pollution of Hollywood, everywhere, we see moral and societal decay. The reason, says author David Long, is that the vast majority of men in America have received tragically inadequate fathering, ranging from an ineffective father to no father at all. This book presents a refreshing vision and a realistic strategy for men to recapture their biblical masculinity.

ISBN 1-56384-047-2 $9.99

New Gods for a New Age

by Richmond Odom

There is a new state religion in this country. The gods of this new religion are Man, Animals, and Earth. Its roots are deeply embedded in Hinduism and other Eastern religions. The author of *New Gods for a New Age* contends that this new religion has become entrenched in our public and political institutions and is being aggressively imposed on all of us.

This humanistic-evolutionary world view has carried great destruction in its path which can be seen in college classrooms where Christianity is belittled, in the courtroom where good is called evil and evil is called good, and in government where the self-interest of those who wield political power is served as opposed to the common good.

The Liberal Contradiction

by Dale A. Berryhill

Why are liberals who took part in student demonstrations in the 1960s now trying to stop Operation Rescue from using the very same tactics? Liberalism claims to advocate some definite moral positions: racism and sexism are wrong; tolerance is right; harming the environment is wrong; protecting it is right. But, contemporary liberalism is undermining its own moral foundation. It contends that its positions are morally right and the opposites are wrong, while at the same time, it denies that a moral law (right and wrong) exists. This is the **Liberal Contradiction** and it leads to many ludicrous (and laughable) inconsistencies.

ISBN 1-56384-055-3 $9.99